FAITH MATTERS

STANDING ON THE THRESHOLD OF EXPECTATION

BY JUDITH L. BUTLER

Copyright © 2016 by Judith L. Butler

Faith Matters
Standing on the Threshold of Expectation
by Judith L. Butler

Printed in the United States of America.

ISBN 9781498476362

All rights reserved solely by the author. The author guarantees all contents are original and do not infringe upon the legal rights of any other person or work. No part of this book may be reproduced in any form without the permission of the author. The views expressed in this book are not necessarily those of the publisher.

Unless otherwise indicated, Scripture quotations taken from he New American Standard Bible, Copyright ©1960, 1962, 1963, 1968, 1971, 1972, 1973, 1975, 1977, 1995 by The Lockman Foundation. Used by permission. www.Lockman.org.

Scripture quotations labeled KJV are from the King James Version of the Bible.

Cover Photo © 2016 by Judith L. Butler

Editing Assistance
Royalene Doyle
doylewrites@comcast.net

www.xulonpress.com

Judith L. Butler

Dedication

In Memory of
Vincent Braner and Edrie Braner,
my parents who have gone on to be with the Lord,
I dedicate this book to them for the years they were
entrusted with the care and upbringing of my two sisters
and myself.

As I look back on those earlier years, I am still a bit overwhelmed by the extraordinary compassion they demonstrated. There was seldom a time that I can recall when there wasn't a friend or relative living with us. Their doors were always open to whoever needed a place to live—for whatever reason—even if it meant for years-on-end. Our home remained peaceful no matter how many took up residence under our roof. My sisters and I now cherish and hold these memories dear to our hearts.

Acknowledgments

To my Father God in Heaven, His Son Jesus Christ, and the Holy Spirit, I thank You for the awesome Grace that You have bestowed upon my life! It is my prayer that this book does not fall short of Your intentions when You spoke these words to me: *"I want you to write a book and call it,* **Faith Matters***."* May it supernaturally reach every man, woman, and child, who You have foreseen from Your Throne Room, to bring them the life-change You have planned for them. May each person realize that You are here with us always and forever <u>attuned</u> to every heart's desire You have planted within us, Your creation. As each person reads this book may they come to experience Your great and awesome Love for them and Your willingness to provide for them <u>above measure</u> as they are being shown by Your Spirit how to press in to know You more fully.

To my editor, Royalene Doyle: I thank you for your encouragement from the beginning, for your conviction and continual confirmation that the two of us were divinely connected for such a time as this—to work on this book as a joint effort. I thank you for your persistence in seeing this work through to completion in Holy Spirit "hand and glove" fashion. It has been *sheer JOY* working with you.

To my friend, Stephen Bateman: I thank you for the many hours you set aside from your busy schedule to assist me with the proofreading of this manuscript along with your most valuable support in this venture. You are a true friend, indeed.

To all my friends who consented to share their stories in this book as well as the many ministries that have contributed indirectly into my life from time to time of which I have also shared in this book — my sincerest appreciation.

To my three children, Suzanne, Brenda, and Jason: I am proud of each one of you and am so blessed to have you by my side. I stay amazed at each of your ways of living out your Faith and living life to the fullest. Each of you demonstrate such a keen sensitivity to the needs of those around you, and your individually unique desires to explore new things — viewing life as an adventure — is a blessing to us all.

INTRODUCTION

THE THOUGHTS OF GOD'S MIND and the intents of God's Heart at Creation were then—and still are today—for **good** and not for evil. For His *Kingdom Purposes*, He chose to give us **free will**, the personal freedom to obey or disobey the voice of our Creator. Of our own volition, we may choose to act as He directs us—or not. And, so it is that I have listened to the Holy Spirit and must step out in obedience with His mandate to write this book. There is too much at stake for me—and for you—if I were to ignore this window of opportunity. **TIME is of the essence** to BE the Church of His Intent—to BE *agents* in the Kingdom of God.

To all who have been singled out by the *finger of GOD* to read this book, I believe that you are already among those who make up the BODY OF CHRIST—The Church. However, there may be a few Readers who are not yet Believers but have been drawn to this book by the Holy Spirit. You are ALL being invited to come along with me as we delve into some of the numerous and various ways that God speaks to *His people* through His Word, particularly what the Scriptures say about visions, dreams, parables, puns, and the myriad of other ways the HOLY SPIRIT desires to *communicate with the saints.* His intent is to bring us into Family Relationship and equip us with the necessary and sufficient weaponry to **triumph in spiritual warfare** as He brings restoration to the BODY OF CHRIST.

Impending war and economic calamity is threatening all nations as the world is being moved ever deeper into **darkness.** Evil has become reinterpreted as good, and our foundational godly laws are being altered accordingly; irrespective of anyone's moral or ethical standards.

In the midst of all this, and with the increase in natural disasters that have been prophesied in the Bible—famines, pestilences, earthquakes in different places, and more troubled times leading up to CHRIST'S RETURN—could it be that GOD IS AWAKENING His army to take the offensive, pursuing the enemy in spiritual warfare from the standpoint of Christ's finished work on the Cross? Could it be that GOD is saying, *"Step up to the plate now and take back everything the enemy has stolen from you."* Is it not in GOD'S PLAN that HIS CHURCH must BE the GLORIOUS BRIDE she was meant to be upon JESUS' RETURN? This can only be accomplished through the *working of the HOLY SPIRIT.* Will HE *automatically* guide us and direct us if we have been *neglecting to develop listening ears to hear what the HOLY SPIRIT is saying to us?*

There is hope! The CHURCH is being offered opportunities to experience greater and greater degrees of *light* which have been and continue to be made available to us through the AWESOME AND EXTENDED ABUNDANCE OF GOD'S GRACE. However, I must bear witness that the **majority of church members of all denominations** are being guided more by their *natural minds* than by the Holy Spirit. When we hear people saying, "God said this to me," and "God said that;" what they are usually saying isn't any different than what their own internal thoughts, opinions, and human perception have come up with. Chances are that they are being *misguided* and *deceived* by the rulers of darkness while being kept in a state of <u>*spiritual unawareness—spiritually asleep.*</u>

Are we not at a critical time and place where we need to be accurately discerning what the SPIRIT OF THE LORD is saying? Shouldn't learning to *hear* the directions of the Holy Spirit be *first and foremost in the hearts of all believers?* Don't we need to know where we are in our walk with the LORD? Shouldn't the priority in the lives of each of us be to know *beyond any shadow of doubt* what GOD is doing in our lives, what GOD is up to, and where we fit into GOD'S agenda both individually and corporately within His Church?

FOR THIS PURPOSE, there are those whom GOD has been raising up to fulfill their present-day roles as apostles, seers, prophets, preachers, teachers—yes, and writers, too. Our **focus** must always *remain on HIM,* and our ears open for HIS GUIDANCE. God has advanced many of these uniquely gifted individuals <u>to levels that only they have an understanding of</u> and they are continually being given increasing clarity and revelation. Others are just beginning to step into the water and reach for a **helping hand** to pull them into their own calling which may be to function in the full capacity of GOD'S **Special Forces group of "Water Walkers."**

We have been brought here—**born into this time**—as dramatic changes are taking place all around the world. **HE waits *for us to speak what He's given us to speak so that the world will know Who it is Who accomplishes those things.*** Yet, how will we <u>know</u> what we are to speak (or write) if our ears are not open to hear what the SPIRIT OF THE LORD is saying to us?

The LORD has told His Church again and again that it must <u>function in unity</u> as a <u>body</u>. To do so, it must *listen* and *hear* with ears that have been *trained in HOLY GHOST sensitivity*. So it is in this context that you are offered the information and examples contained within the pages of this book as a challenge to stir up—even ignite—a greater desire to hear the Lord's voice wherein and into whatsoever His voice might be speaking.

JESUS spent hours in *daily prayer*, often *praying into the night*, listening to His Father's instructions then telling the believers to go out and do the same. JESUS said, **"For I did not speak on My own initiative, but the Father Himself who sent Me has given Me a commandment as to what to say and what to speak."** (John 12:49)

Then JESUS said, **"These things I have spoken to you while abiding with you. But the Helper, the Holy Spirit, whom the Father will send in My name, He will teach you all things, and bring to your remembrance all that I said to you."** (John 14:25, 26)

Jesus' promise of the arrival of the Holy Spirit, as our Helper, is also confirmed in the Book of Acts. One hundred and twenty (120) believers who were in one accord in prayer and supplication—including the women and Mary, the mother of Jesus, and His brethren—waited as they had been instructed. *"When the day of Pentecost had come, they were all together in one place. And suddenly there came from heaven a noise like a violent rushing wind, and it filled the whole house where they were sitting. And there appeared to them tongues as of fire distributing themselves, and they rested on each one of them. And they were all filled with the Holy Spirit and began to speak with other tongues,* **as the Spirit** *was giving them utterance"* (Acts 2:1-4)

THIS PROMISE reaches out to us today! In Acts 2:39, we are clearly told that the Holy Spirit's place in our lives is meant *for you and your children and for* **all who are far off** (all future generations)

Introduction

as many as the Lord our God will call to Himself. So if ever there was a day when those in the BODY OF CHRIST need to call out to the Holy Spirit for His HELP, it is in this generation! It is unmistakably evident that we need to <u>walk the tightest rope ever</u> **over** what is transpiring **in the world**. For this to become reality **within the Church** today we need the Holy Spirit to show us <u>how to run the tightest ship ever,</u> especially when it comes to recognizing what is being spoken to us by HIM.

There is great need of—and room for—the Church to <u>accept</u> the leading of the HOLY SPIRIT and learn of HIS WAYS. This book—birthed in hours of prayer and an open heart—offers observations that I pray will be informative, uplifting, encouraging, and refreshing. May it also reveal a <u>*perspective of GOD*</u> that you might not have seen before.

Respectfully,
    Judith Butler

FYI: Throughout these pages I have used <u>underlining</u>, CAPITALIZATIONS, and **bold** highlights to emphasize my focus within a chapter and/or the essence of Scripture quotes as they have amplified my personal understanding. It is my hope that this process will also encourage you in the *personal* study and awakening of God's Word within you.

Table of Contents

Dedication v
Acknowledgements vii
Introduction ix
Chapter One: *Know Your Divine Destiny* 17
Chapter Two: *Matters of Faith* 29
Chapter Three: *Each Has a Role to Play* 43
Chapter Four: *Putting Angels to Work* 65
Chapter Five: *The Spirit Makes Intercession* 87
Chapter Six: *Wisdom in Relationships* 109
Chapter Seven: *People Connections ~ Reconnections* 141
Chapter Eight: *Our Covenant of Faith* 163
Ministries and Reading Resources: 193

Chapter One

Know Your Divine Destiny

IT WAS A NICE SUNNY DAY when my friend, Janice, called to see if I would ride to Peoria with her to pick up her sister at the airport. I was happy for any opportunity to spend time with this friend since she was living forty miles away from me, and we seldom got to see each other. We got lost going to the airport and lost going back out of town. We even had to stop at one place to ask directions because few people at that time owned a GPS system.

That evening, Prophetess Juanita Bynum[1] was giving a teaching on television about **knowing our Divine destinies.**

I had a dream the same night that picked up where Janice and I were on our way home and in the dream Janice was driving just as she had been earlier that same afternoon. We seemed well on our way home, driving at normal speed in the left hand lane, when I suddenly saw an exit ramp that we were supposed to be taking. By the time I realized that we were supposed to be exiting the highway on that ramp, we were about to miss it totally. Nevertheless, we went for it.

---

[1] Juanita Bynum: American Televangelist

We cut across the right hand lane but missed the actual entrance point onto the exit which meant we were crossing over gravel barely making it onto the ramp. Still attempting to reduce the speed to the posted recommendations, but not quite there yet, I could feel the centrifugal force of the car hugging the pavement. Then I heard these words, "Hug Divine destiny."

My immediate thought was a question. "How do I hug Divine destiny?" Isn't that what you would have asked?

The next thing I heard was, "Call out to God for everything."

One thing about *dreams* is that we have no control over what we hear or how we respond. Our awareness of where we are in the natural realm, or what is transpiring around us, is temporarily suspended. This is also true of **visions** from God.

Have you ever told someone about a dream you had, followed by their response that equates your dream to something you ate before you went to bed or something you just *happened* to be thinking about when you went to sleep? What if it **was** God's message to you in the night season? Will you **miss** His message by rationalizing it was *just an ordinary dream?*

It says in Job 33:14-18, *"Indeed God speaks once, or twice, yet no one notices it. In a dream, a vision of the night, when sound sleep falls on men, while they slumber in their beds,* **then He opens the ears of men, and seals their instruction, that He may turn man aside from his conduct, and keep man from pride; He keeps back his soul from the pit, and his life from passing over into Sheol."**

And in verses 29 and 30 *"Behold, God does all these oftentimes with men,* **to bring back his soul from the pit,** *that he may be enlightened with the light of life."* Doesn't that make us want to pay more attention to our dreams?

What if Joseph (husband of the virgin, Mary) had ignored the dream God gave him where the angel of the Lord was telling him to *fear not* taking Mary as his wife? Within the confines of his own natural logic, Joseph was planning to send Mary away secretly, not wanting to disgrace her. However, because an angel appeared to him in a dream; he was *nudged* back into his Divine destiny.

What if the Wise Men (highly educated scholars from the East) paid no attention to any of the dreams God gave them? What if they disregarded the *dream* God gave them to not return to Herod?

What if Joseph gave no heed to the angel who appeared to him in a dream telling him to take Mary and Jesus and flee into Egypt? Or—at the dream-directed time—to return to Israel?

> (Matthew 2:13) *"Now when they had gone, behold, an angel of the Lord appeared to Joseph in a dream and said, "Get up! Take the Child and His mother, and flee to Egypt, and remain there until I tell you; for Herod is about to search for the Child, to destroy Him."*

> (Matthew 2:20) *"Get up, take the Child and His mother, and go into the land of Israel; for those who sought the Child's life are dead."*

Joseph got up, took the Child and His mother and came into the land of Israel but heard that Archelaus was reigning over Judea in place of his father, Herod, and was afraid to go there.

> (Matthew 2:23, 24) *"....Then after being warned by God in a dream, he left for the regions of Galilee, and*

came and lived in a city called Nazareth. This was to fulfill what was spoken through the prophets, 'He shall be called a Nazarene.'"

Approximately 30 years later we meet Saul of Tarsus (a Pharisee, educated in Judaism beyond most of his peers, and persecutor of Christians). He was definitely on the wrong track as long as he was pursuing the capture of the disciples of the early Church. He even encouraged the stoning of Stephen. Then God's *supernatural Divine intervention* met him on the road to Damascus. Within three days of Saul's conversion experience, the Lord spoke to His disciple Ananias **in a vision** and told him to go to the street which was called Straight and inquire of Judas for this man by the name of Saul. Not only had Saul been praying <u>and seen a vision</u> of a man by the name of Ananias coming in and laying his hands on him that he might regain his sight, but Ananias was also shown that Saul was to be filled with the Holy Spirit through the same laying on of Ananias' hands that healed him. <u>Both these men were being given *visions* from the Lord quite possibly simultaneously.</u> Ananias was already walking in *his Divine destiny*, and he was commissioned of the Lord to help get Saul started on the path that was in *GOD'S HEAVENLY BLUEPRINT FOR HIM.*

The Apostle Luke tells us of the *vision* that Peter was given when he went on the rooftop to pray (Acts 10:9-16). Here we can see how messages from God can be very closely related to our natural lives because Peter became very hungry and would have eaten, but the meal was still in the preparation stages. The Word of God says that while they were making preparations for their meal, Peter fell into a trance. Within this trance state (or sleep, perhaps even dozing off in a half awake/half asleep state.)

"…..He saw the sky opened up, and an object like a great sheet coming down, lowered by four corners to the ground, and there were in it all kinds of four-footed animals and crawling creatures of the earth and birds of the air. A voice came to him, 'Get up, Peter, kill and eat!' But Peter said, 'By no means, Lord, for I have never eaten anything unholy and unclean.' Again a voice came to him a second time, 'What God has cleansed, no longer consider unholy.' This happened three times, and immediately the object was taken up into the sky.'"

When this vision ended, Peter was greatly perplexed in his mind about what the vision meant when he had seen himself in this vision refusing to eat meat that God had already revealed to him had been cleansed. Then suddenly, before Peter had enough information to see how this parable/message applied to him and his ministry, the Holy Spirit informed him that three men were looking for him, sent to him by the Holy Spirit, and that he was to accompany them without questioning.

Peter went out to these men as the Holy Spirit instructed him to do. Immediately, they began to share with him the details of how Cornelius (a Roman Centurion who believed in the God of Israel) had received Divine direction by an angel of God who appeared to him in a ***vision*** when he was praying in his home in Caesarea. The angel instructed Cornelius to send men to Joppa, find Peter at this house by the sea, and bring Peter back with them.

Peter invited the three men to stay overnight and left with them the next day taking six of his own brethren in Christ with them. By the time they arrived at the home of Cornelius, Peter had a clearer understanding of what the vision he had seen meant and told them, "......*God has shown me that I should not call any man unholy or unclean.*" (Acts 10:28)

<u>When men do their part</u> in performing these roles within God's Divine calling on their lives, God shows up to do His part! While Peter was still explaining the Gospel to the people who had gathered in the house of Cornelius, the Holy Spirit fell upon all who were listening—and they all began to speak with other tongues. Then Peter answered, "*Surely no one can refuse the water for these to be baptized who have received the Holy Spirit just as we did, can he?*" (Acts 10:47)

Peter was referring to the Day of Pentecost. On that day, the original believers—disciples of Jesus—were fervently praying in one accord with supplication, and the Holy Spirit became present in their midst. With tongues of fire visible above their heads and the sound of a mighty rushing wind that filled the whole house, they were anointed with His Power and the ability to speak/be heard in many languages, praising God for His wonderful works!

Even though the languages were being understood, what was actually transpiring was not understood until Peter, himself, stood up in the midst of all of them. He then explained to them in a common language that what they were witnessing was what was spoken of by the prophet Joel:

> "*And it shall be in the last days, God says, that I will pour forth of my Spirit on all mankind; and your sons and your daughters shall prophesy, and your young men shall see visions, and your old men shall*

dream dreams; even on my bondslaves, both men and women, I will in those days pour forth of My Spirit and they shall prophesy. And I will grant wonders in the sky above and signs on the earth below, blood, and fire, and vapor of smoke. The sun will be turned into darkness and the moon into blood, before the great and glorious day of the Lord shall come. And it shall be that everyone who calls on the name of the Lord will be saved." (Acts 2:17-21)

This phenomenon occurred in the beginning of the **last day dispensation** with accounts of believers being added to the Church throughout the entire book of Acts as they received this same Holy Spirit with the same *evidence* of speaking with other tongues and prophesying.

Today, we find ourselves living in the last of this last day dispensation. The same Holy Spirit is being poured out on us as was poured out on them. People who have received this mighty *Baptism of the Holy Spirit* are still being given *visions and dreams* from God, and God continues to raise up Apostles, Prophets, and Seers—right along with Preachers, Teachers, and Evangelists.

God is still speaking to His People in the same like manner because He does not change. Neither does He alter the thing that goes out of His lips. His ways cannot be numbered any more than the sand in the sea can be numbered or the stars in the sky. God does not want us to limit Him when He does not limit us; and the more open we are to all His various ways of communicating with us, the more understanding we are going to have of what His Word is truly saying to us.

Each one of us within the BODY OF CHRIST is meant to be hearing—in our spirits—what the Holy Spirit is saying to each of us. The Word of God contains multiple accounts of how the Holy Spirit spoke to the early Church. These examples in Scripture are meant to release His ways in us so that we become ready, willing and able to bear fruit in our lives—always giving God the Glory for that which we cannot work to accomplish in and of ourselves.

Not many years after the dream I had that I shared in the beginning of this chapter, one of our neighbors was having a problem with his combine malfunctioning and catching the fields on fire. It was about the third time this happened that the fire came closer to where I lived. Fortunately, by this third time, the crops had just been taken out of the fields surrounding my home. Still, with all the stubble left in the fields, the fire raged on, getting much too close for comfort.

I made a phone call to one person in an attempt to hear some news that could ease my mind. I was told not to worry because the fire would not jump the creek. I called a second person and was told the fire had already crossed the creek and was in the field traveling in the direction of my house.

In the country where there are no water lines, the fire fighters have to haul tanks of water to the fields, and they had been fighting this fire all night. The winds had picked up to 35-40 mph which only added to the difficulties. It seemed no time at all when the fire reached the corner of my yard just on the other side of the little country road that bordered both south and west sides of my residence. The grayish black billows of smoke reached as high as the 30-foot tall corn bins.

Black smoke was rolling across my yard, and I could see red fire in the smoke. It was so thick by then that I couldn't detect just where the fire was burning. I knew it was either on one side of the road or the other. There was no time to try to hook up hoses to the outdoor hydrants to wet the roof down or try any other feeble attempt at saving the day for me. So, I did just what I heard in my dream—"Call out to God for everything." I lifted my voice and called out to God to save me.

I was out in my yard, and I raised my hands toward heaven as high up as I could get them and yelled at the top of my voice, **"Dear God, will you please help me?"** Then I ran into the house for just a minute or so and right back out the door. To my amazement, **the wind had changed direction!** It was still blowing at the same velocity, but it was blowing the fire back in the direction it had come from. Praise the Lord for sudden answers to prayer!

A few weeks afterward, I was talking with our propane delivery man about the fire. After I shared my account with him, he told me that he'd spoken with one of the fire fighters who told him that "the strangest thing happened when they were fighting that fire. All of a sudden, the wind totally changed direction and was blowing the fire back upon itself."

In reflecting back on this episode, I am being reminded that every miracle from God is for us to glean from. **His miracles are worthy of Holy Spirit led contemplation, not only for the days to follow, but decades to follow.** Most importantly, should it not be that **praise and thanksgiving** needs to spring up in our hearts at the very thought of how GOD, in His abundance of MERCY toward us, is ever so willing to show Himself alive and present in the midst of our troubling circumstances.

Even as we experience days that may be trouble free, there are those close to us who may be facing giant obstacles. **Praising God and giving God glory is a powerful weapon against the oppressors of our souls that dwell in clouds of deep darkness endeavoring to pull mankind into that same darkness.** Yet God has said that <u>there is no place</u> so deep or dark that His **LOVE** is not deeper still, and His strong right arm is able to deliver us out and set our feet back on solid ground.

Praising God and giving God glory will fill our spiritual houses with HIS PRESENCE. Whether we praise Him in our closets or in the midst of the largest church on earth, we can compare our worship to the Levitical singers who were gathered with one hundred twenty priests to praise God in the Temple that King Solomon built.

> II Chronicles 5:13,14 we can *hear* them: *"...in unison when the trumpeters and the singers were to make themselves heard with one voice to praise and to glorify the Lord, and when they lifted up their voice accompanied by trumpets and cymbals and instruments of music, and when they praised the LORD saying, "He indeed is good for His lovingkindness is everlasting," then the house, the house of the LORD, was filled with a cloud, so that the priests could not stand to minister because of the cloud, for the glory of the LORD filled the house of GOD."*
>
> Then Solomon said in II Chronicles 6:14, *"O Lord, the God of Israel, there is no god like You in heaven or on earth, keeping covenant and showing*

lovingkindness to Your servants who walk before You with all their heart..."

Personal Note based on my understanding: *Visions*, like *dreams*, are seen at times when our awareness of what is transpiring in the natural realm is suspended. We can have visions with words being spoken concerning what we are seeing, or not. What we *see* can be still pictures or moving pictures, and they can also contain words that are **bold print** in various sizes and fonts, in color, or in any other form that the HOLY SPIRIT chooses to present them, depending on the manner which carries the greatest relevance. We can have dreams with visions within the dreams or dreams within dreams. Neither is limited to natural laws that pertain to the universe. For example, we may be shown a sunrise over water next to a power plant when the sun neither rises nor sets in the direction of that specific power plant. The variety can be as diverse as the stars in the sky or the sand in the sea when they are of a spiritual nature because they originate with GOD, and GOD holds the keys to their interpretations. Interpretations of dreams and/or visions may come to us as we prayerfully press in to come to understanding, but not always. Sometimes more needs to transpire in our lives and then we look back on the dream. At other times, interpretive clarifications need to wait for God's timing. We must keep ourselves in check so that we don't look at all dreams as *spiritual dreams*. It is, however, quite possible that many of the dreams we've dismissed are spiritual in content. Through prayer and open hearts and minds toward the Holy Spirit, He will guide and counsel us as He makes all things clear.

Chapter Two

Matters of Faith

WHEN LISTENING to what people are saying, it is easy to pick up on the fact that there are many different ideas about what *faith* is. Some refer to faith as the religious affiliation or church denomination they are connected with and the belief system they maintain within these various denominations. Others refer to faith in the way they have personally developed their beliefs in God based on personal experience. Others still, believe that God does exist or that God is in control of everything that happens to us throughout our lives, yet no personal relationship could exist between God and humans. In other words, many of us are sailing through life with the notion that we have no personal decision to make, or role to play, in what is to transpire in our lives and no control of the outcome because God is the one who is in control, and He alone determines the outcome.

Whether one can fit his *faith definition* into any of these categories mentioned above, or whether one's faith definition is something of a totally different concept, we need to ascertain the meaning of what faith <u>really is</u> based exclusively upon God's Word. Each of us needs to be willing to redefine our own ideology about faith in the light of the Gospel; to allow God's Infallible Word to change any wrong notion, whether dealing with large or small erroneous concepts. We are either ready to allow our thinking to be conformed to the Word of God, or we will continue to twist and turn the Word of God to fit into our own personal theology. This second option is a dangerous one.

> In the Apostle Paul's letter to the Romans (12:2,3) he writes, "***And do not be conformed to this world, but be transformed by the renewing of your mind, so that you may prove what the will of God is .... to think so as to have sound judgment, as God has allotted to each a measure of faith.***"

It is my desire that we will all be open to change, no matter where our thoughts might differ from the interpretation of Scriptures, but especially where we find the word "faith" **defined**. Is it too much to assume that the Holy Spirit had something to do with this book coming into your hands for such a time as this? This is a time when we, as believers, need to be on the same page, at least as close to the same page as the followers of Jesus in the early Church.

Each one of us can contemplate taking one giant step into a new thing that God has for us, only to experience a sense of fear, hesitancy, or doubt in our own ability to sustain ourselves in that place. However, if we had full assurance in our hearts that this move involved God and His full assurance that He was not only able but willing and faithful to hold us up in this new place, wouldn't we be bolder to make the move? How many of us are in this place in our faith walk? How many of us are secure enough in our faith to know beyond any shadow of doubt that God is going to be there to enable us to switch into *supernatural gear* if that is what it is going to take in order for us to make it in the new place He has for us? Are we ready to follow Him there?

In Matthew 8:23-26, the disciples followed Jesus into a ship. While Jesus slept in the ship, a storm arose to the point that the ship was covered with waves. When the disciples woke Jesus, asking Him if He didn't care that they perish, Jesus asked them why they were so fearful. Then He added, *"you men of little faith?"* He instantly rebuked the wind, and the sea became calm. Have you ever wondered whether Jesus would have even asked that question—as if rebuking them for not exercising even their "little faith"—if it had not been **possible** for His disciples themselves to rebuke the wind and let Jesus go right on sleeping?

In Matthew 14:29-31, Jesus told Peter to come out of the ship. Yet Peter became fearful because of the strong wind, and Jesus stretched out His hand and saved him from sinking. Then Jesus said to Peter, *"You of little faith, why did you doubt?"*

Jesus made a strong point with His words—telling all of us that we must have faith in Him. I've learned that to be in faith and also to stay in faith requires an ability to walk in the supernatural power of God. To rely on our own strength is an indication that we are in doubt—that **we doubt our personal faith in the Lord and may even doubt His power.** Our own natural strength was never meant to sustain us through any given situation. It is His loving kindness and mercy, given to us *new every morning* that builds our faith. (See Lamentations 3:22-24)

So we can ask ourselves again, "What kind of faith do I possess? Do the concepts about faith given here match my own personal definition of faith?" Because if it doesn't, then—based on just these passages of Scripture—what we have been assuming was *a walk of faith* may not have been a ***walk of faith*** at all.

In Matthew 17:14-21 and Mark 9:17-27, we can read of a situation when a certain man came to Jesus and told Him that His disciples were not able to cure his son. Jesus then rebuked the devil, and the devil departed out of the child. When the disciples asked Jesus why they could not cast out the devil, Jesus told them it was because of their **unbelief.** They needed to be praying **and** fasting in order for them to have the faith to cast out **that** devil! Jesus said, *"But this **kind** does not go out except by prayer and fasting."* This account gives credence to the fact that **faith is a powerful gift from God and it produces supernatural results.**

My own faith has been an ever-developing journey over many years and continues to grow. One specific example—of faith producing supernatural results—centers around a real estate transaction that proved to be impossible to complete without accessing the *supernatural power* of God.

About midway through my 25 years in real estate, I received a commission check in the amount of $1400. Being true to what I thought was my faith commitment (tithe) to the Lord I came home and immediately wrote out a check in the amount of $140 to send to one of the ministries I had been supporting. Up until then, my giving was based more on obligation to give of the tithe as set forth in Malachi 3:18. I was not yet to the stage of wrapping expectation around the seed I was sowing even though it also says in Malachi 3:10, *"Bring the whole tithe into the storehouse, so that there may be food in My house, and test Me now in this,' says the LORD of hosts, 'if I will not open for you the windows of heaven and pour out for you a blessing until it overflows.'"* Our seed needs to be *wrapped* with what the Word of God is saying about our harvest of the seed being sown when it is being sown in the rich soil of God's Kingdom.

It just happened that I received four additional mailings from various other ministries that I supported periodically. This was one of those times when I figured all these other ministries were going to send me envelopes in the mail again the next month so I would just wait until the next month to give to them. Subsequently, I tossed them all into the trash can and proceeded to clean out my refrigerator because garbage pickup was early the next morning.

I made it to bed that night with my head at rest on the pillow when suddenly I was being shown a flashback *vision of myself* tossing those ministry envelopes into the trash can. At that same instant, the word **"insignificant"** was being spoken to my spirit. Clearly, the HOLY SPIRIT was showing me that I was treating those ministries as being insignificant. I knew I either had to crawl out of bed to go get them then or set the alarm for early the next morning if I was going to be obedient to what the HOLY SPIRIT was showing me. After stewing about it for a few minutes, I decided to get back out of bed and go find them. They were somewhere in that trash can and I didn't relish the thought of how far down I was going to have to sift before I found them, but I did.

Rather small amounts ended up going to these ministries when the initial tithe amount wasn't a whole lot bigger. It takes greater faith to let go of the little we have than it does for someone who has acquired much to give out of his abundance.

> In Mark 12:43, 44, **we are shown the heart of a person with deep faith.** *"Calling His disciples to Him, He said to them, 'Truly I say to you, this poor widow put in more than all the contributors to the treasury; for they all put in out of their surplus, but she, out of her poverty, put in all she owned, all she had to live on.'"* This same event is recorded again in Luke 21:2-4.

At this same time two of my children were in need of a new place to live and I knew I had to help them. Thinking I would run a casual search on the computer in case a suitable house might be listed in the system, I couldn't help but take notice of a beautiful home that had been appraised way above anything affordable when it was first listed on the open market. I was shocked to see that it had been reduced in price numerous enough times that it was now within my grasp. I called my son to meet me at the property, and we both loved it!

This historical home sat with only one other house on a 40-acre tract of land just off from the Capitol Building during the turn of the century. Both homes belonged to the same family. All this area had been developed over the past one hundred years with this 3,000 square-foot structure now situated on four lots with a detached 3-car garage and a large parking lot. The style was Old English Shingle Style architecture with a screened-in porch that ran the full depth of one side of the home, and it was loaded with character.

I couldn't wait to get back to the office to write my offer, only to discover that there were two other offers presented to the listing office ahead of mine.

The home had belonged to a judge who had moved to California to live with his son. **His son came from California and—for some reason known only to him—he accepted my offer over the others.** Then he went back to California. My broker, who was currently chairperson of our local Historical Site Commission, was so excited about the fact that I was purchasing this home that **he announced it at our next staff meeting!**

I felt positive that any bank was going to give me a 95% loan because of all the equity in this home, but I had a surprise coming. After numerous calls to local banks, I was being told by all of them that they would require a 20% down payment because it was not going to be my own live-in residence. I didn't have 20% to put down.

Things had happened so rapidly that I hadn't taken the time to pray about this decision and I now wondered if I had gotten out of step with the HOLY SPIRIT. If so, it seemed I could end up without that home and with egg on my face in front of everybody. I began immediately to pray Scriptures that were pertinent to this circumstance; that God's people will never be ashamed. At the same time, I called the strongest prayer warrior I knew to stand with me in faith and confidence that God would remove any obstacles to our successful purchase of this home.

Subsequently, that night I had a *dream* where a little girl was prophesying to me. She appeared to be my little girl although I had never seen her before. She was saying, "Thus saith the LORD, 'Let me override you in this like I have so many other times.'" I woke up from the dream thinking, "Yes, LORD! Please do!"

We hear a number of preachers these days who recommend to the BODY OF CHRIST that we develop a habit of **working the Word of God!** By this, they imply that it is good practice to read the Scriptures and talk to GOD about what His Word is saying to us. In this instance, I began to **work the dream.** I began to talk with God about the dream. "LORD, this dream had to have been from You. You would not have given me this dream if You were not going to do what You told me You were going to do. I believe You are telling me that You have a way where I have no way." I was moving into **expectancy mode.**

Three days went by, and it seemed that Heaven was being very silent. Is anything happening? I recalled how demonic forces in the spirit realm are dispatched to intercept what God sends to us, and angels war against them on our behalf. I knew my prayer warrior was doing battle with and for me, and I was doing much warring in the spirit myself. (The topic of **warring-in-the-spirit** will be expanded upon in future chapters.)

After three days, I needed to hear from the LORD more specifically about just **where—precisely where—**this money was coming from. When we are being led to pray **specific prayers,** we need to expect **specific answers.** Ecclesiastes 5:1, 2 cautions us to be more ready to listen than to speak when we go before the LORD, because GOD is in Heaven and we are on earth, so who are we to tell GOD anything? My prayer was brief and to the point, "LORD, where is the money coming from?"

Then I began to pray in the spirit because the best thing about *praying in tongues* is that it helps us to hear with our spiritual ears, and it enables us to see with our spiritual eyes.

What I saw was a *vision* of the word, "**WOODLAKE**," in big <u>bold print</u>. Woodlake was the name of the subdivision where our parents had lived. We were being told by both the attorney and the executor of their estate that we would **not** be receiving any proceeds from the sale of their home because it was going to have to go toward inheritance taxes. However; because I saw the name of the subdivision when I was praying, I called both of them to see if there was any change in that status. When questioned by the executor as to just how much money I was talking about, he responded that **I <u>would be</u> receiving that exact amount the next week. Praise the LORD! Because of a dream, what once seemed impossible had become "exactly" possible.** Now I was able to obtain financing on the balance, and we <u>finalized</u> the purchasing of that fabulous home!

The closing was in the month of October and when Easter rolled around the next year, I decided that it would be a nice gesture to send an Easter bouquet to my friend and prayer warrior who I had asked to pray with me concerning the financing for that house. Her name was Callie so I called and ordered some *Calla Lilies* to be delivered to her home on Saturday, the day before Easter Sunday.

Callie called me after they arrived to share with me that she was planning to have her family over for Easter dinner and wanted something in the way of a centerpiece for her dinner table. She'd gone to the basement to see if there was anything from Christmas that she might be able to convert to a centerpiece for Easter. She couldn't find anything that would work so she proceeded back up the stairs. Just as she reached the top of the stairs the doorbell rang, and there was the centerpiece for her Easter dinner table being delivered right to her door.

Perhaps as some of you are reading this, you may be wondering why I wasn't believing GOD to bring me enough to cover the full amount to pay for this home. I can honestly say—and believe—that if my faith had been developed to receive the total amount to cover the full purchase, I would have set out to ask GOD for the full amount. My faith wasn't there yet and even if it had been, that may not have been God's plan <u>or</u> it may have fallen into His <u>permissive will</u> as opposed to His <u>perfect will</u>. His perfect will for us would be that we walk in total freedom from debt because that is what was provided for us through Jesus' death on the Cross.

> In Matthew 6:33, Jesus said, *"But seek first His Kingdom and His Righteousness, and all these things will be added to you."*
>
> In Luke 12:24, Jesus said, *"Consider the ravens, for they neither sow nor reap; they have no storeroom nor barn, and yet God feeds them; how much more valuable you are than the birds!"*
>
> Then in Romans 1:16, 17, *"For I am not ashamed of the Gospel, for it is the power of God for salvation to everyone who believes, to the Jew first and also to the Greek. For in it the righteousness of God is revealed from faith to faith."*

Can we not assume that if we are to first seek His Kingdom and His Righteousness, which is revealed from *faith to faith*, that indeed these accompanying promises of God will be realized in same like manner, as we go from faith to faith?

> In Mark 10: 29, 30 we read where, *"Jesus said, 'Truly I say to you, there is no one who has left house or brothers or sisters or mother or father or children or farms, for My sake and for the Gospel's sake, but that he will receive a hundred times as much now in the present age, houses and brothers and sisters and mothers and children and farms, along with persecutions; and in the age to come, eternal life.'"*

When Jesus came into the district of Caesarea Philippi and was asking His disciples, *"Who do people say that the Son of Man is,"* he asked Simon Peter, *"Who do you say that I am?"* When Peter answered, *"You are the Christ, the Son of the living God,"* Jesus told him that flesh and blood had not revealed this to him, but His Father which was in heaven.

In Matthew 16:18, 19, Jesus continued, *"I also say to you that you are Peter, and upon this rock I will build My church; and the gates of Hades will not overpower it. I will give you the keys of the kingdom of heaven; and whatever you bind on earth shall have been bound in heaven, and whatever you loose on earth shall have been loosed in heaven."* When we, as believers, <u>bind</u> the wasted years and <u>loose</u> the blessing flow, doors are opened to us to **become overcomers.**

So the question remains, "How big is our GOD?" Are WE the ones who limit GOD? I believe that GOD would say to us, **"Don't limit ME. I don't limit you."**

A Practice Run

Years prior to the house-purchase-event, at a time when I was attempting to rebound from the complications and financial hardship of losing practically everything in a divorce, I took a job as a salesperson in a local furniture store. I had fallen into a state of "deferred hope." However, after spending enough time in the Word of God to build a small arsenal of Scriptures to back me, I was ready to put faith into *action*. It seemed a good idea to me to come up with a **faith project** merely because I couldn't remember when I had last seen GOD show up on the scene.

The furniture store had a half-price sale on a sofa I liked. The sofa, with two matching table lamps, came to a thousand dollars. I stepped out in faith and *financed them*. Sometimes it takes faith to charge something because we have to believe we are going to be able to come up with the monthly payments. Of course, this is not GOD's best for us so I am not recommending this to anyone.

I was notified by the store manager the next day that it was a conflict of interest for me to use their finance company because I was an employee, and this was a privilege only allotted to customers. However, they had already approved me for the financing so they told me I could charge the furniture this time, but no more. All the more reason for me to believe GOD to have this charge paid off in three days. This would make for even a better *faith project—one* thousand dollars coming to me from Heaven in three days.

I started telling people that a thousand dollars was on its way to me from Heaven, and it's going to be here in three days. The third day arrived and mid-afternoon I went to the mailbox to get my thousand dollars. The phone was ringing as I came back into the house so I picked up the phone and was telling my friend on the other end of the line that a thousand dollars was on its way to me from Heaven arriving that day. Still on the phone with her and sifting through my mail, I came upon an envelope from out-of-state. Inside that envelope was a check in the amount of $1,000. The next words to my friend on the other end of the line were, "You are not going to believe this, MaryAnn, but I am looking at a check in the amount of $1,000!" It had come from a couple who had heard by way of the grapevine that I was going through a rough time. **Praise the LORD!** I had a new testimony to the **faithfulness of GOD!**

Sometimes we need to jump-start our faith. We need to get enough of the Word of God inside of us to have a solid place to push off from and the Word of GOD is as solid as the Rock, Himself, in the spirit realm. That "deferred hope" attitude I'd fallen into was gone. I had spent enough time in the Word of God to build a small arsenal of Scriptures to strengthen me, and I was then able to move beyond some of the damages with a "ray of hope" that God could bring *change to my future IF I could keep on moving in this new, God-led direction.*

<u>**Personal Notes**</u>: GOD is not moved by our needs—otherwise we would all have all of our needs met all the time. What moves the hand of GOD is **faith.** Jesus confirms this when talking to the two blind men who were healed...

> Matthew 9:27-30.... *"As Jesus went on from there, two blind men followed Him, crying out, 'Have mercy on us, Son of David!' When He entered the house, the blind men came up to Him, and Jesus said to them,* **'Do you believe that I am able to do this?'** *They*

> said to Him, 'Yes, Lord.' Then He touched their eyes, saying, **'It shall be done to you according to your faith.'** And their eyes were opened."

As we keep His Word in front of us—and in our faith-filled hearts—to the point that our actions are springing out of the Word of GOD, that is when we will activate God's hand on our behalf.

> Psalm 37:4: "Delight yourself in the LORD; And He will give you the desires of your heart."

This is further confirmed in His Word in Philippians 4:19, "And my God will supply all your needs according to His riches in glory in Christ Jesus."

We can stand on this promise by faith.

> Further, we must understand that, "...... without faith it is impossible to please Him: for he who comes to God must believe that He is, and that He is a rewarder of those who seek Him." Hebrews 11:6

Faith—growing faith—is a vital part of our growing relationship with God and even when circumstances or people speak otherwise, *someone must be standing in faith.*

Chapter Three

Each Has a Role to Play

We **need to pray** every day and believe GOD to see change if we are to be *ambassadors* for GOD's Kingdom purposes. Based on Paul's words to the Church of Corinth—in II Corinthians 5:20—we have already been made ambassadors of Christ through **reconciliation,** when Jesus who knew no sin, became sin on our behalf.

> II Corinthians 5: 18-20 says, *"Now all these things are from God, who reconciled us to Himself through Christ and gave us the ministry of reconciliation, namely, that God was in Christ reconciling the world to Himself, not counting their trespasses against them, and He has committed to us the word of reconciliation. Therefore, we are ambassadors for Christ, as though God were making an appeal through us; we beg you on behalf of Christ, be reconciled to God."*

It is <u>when we accept Jesus and His reconciliation work</u> that we become ambassadors. If you are like me, I don't feel like an ambassador, nor do I look like an ambassador. Yet if Paul is calling us ambassadors, then ambassadors we are. According to Webster's Dictionary, an ambassador is <u>any authorized messenger or representative—one who stands for or represents a particular belief, set of values, or culture</u>; **an ambassador for change**.

Every place where Jesus went, people's lives were changed. Likewise, every place where the Apostles went, lives were changed. Subsequently, as souls were added to the Church through the centuries, even more change became evident. Today—where you and I are concerned—the work continues through the <u>gifts</u> of the Holy Spirit, the <u>power</u> of the Holy Spirit, and the <u>anointing</u> of the Holy Spirit. God continues to bring about miraculous cause and effect!

Now more than ever we need to be calling out to God for Him to strengthen that which He has wrought in us and for us. We need to slide all <u>worldly systems</u> aside and come out of <u>lukewarm</u> mindsets toward the things of God. This might sound like a big order to fulfill, but we were never meant to accomplish any great things FOR God by our own human efforts. We were meant to stay small in our own eyes so that God can accomplish mighty things **through us.** We can believe God to lift us up to *more than we can be* when we are being diligent to attend to His Word which *empowers us*. We have all the **hosts of heaven** to assist us in this awesome endeavor to turn the world upside down for CHRIST, just as the early Church believers had at their disposal.

> Psalms 103:20, *"Bless the Lord, you His angels, Mighty in strength, who perform His word, Obeying the voice of His word!"*

Angels are not only ON ASSIGNMENT, but angels are HANDING OUT ASSIGNMENTS! Some examples of angels giving directions to people are: When an angel spoke to Joseph in a *dream* about accepting Mary as his wife (Matthew 1:20); when an angel spoke to Philip directing him to meet a man from Ethiopia on the road (Acts 8:26); and when an angel appeared to Cornelius in a *vision* (Acts 10:1-8).

So, how is it that we are to recognize ourselves within the process of changing events? Do we have open eyes and unstopped ears to hear what the SPIRIT OF THE LORD is saying to us? Are we prepared to discern they are angels from Heaven and **listen** should an angel give us directions? Do we have open eyes and unstopped ears to discern what is transpiring in the unseen realm? Can we pick up on how the truths of God's Word are working from the inside out in changing us so that we might be the vessels God can work through to change the world around us?

> Ephesians 2:10 tells us, "*.....we are His workmanship, created in Christ Jesus for good works, which God prepared beforehand so that <u>we would walk in them</u>.*"

Each of us has a unique role to play. Together we make up the BODY OF CHRIST. Among these individual members, there are differences in administrations, but the <u>same</u> <u>LORD</u> "*who works all things in all persons*" (I Corinthians 12:6).

The entire passage of Scriptures in I Corinthians 23 describes how members of CHRIST'S CHURCH were <u>created and designed to function as a whole</u>. We should be endeavoring to operate like a smooth, well-oiled machine, with each member showing care one for another. The Word says if one member suffers, all members suffer; and if one member is honored, all rejoice. Promotion (positioning) comes from GOD, and it is GOD who chooses who He raises up and who He sits down at any given time.

<u>Sad But True</u>

Unfortunately, I believe there are many pastors standing up behind pulpits on earth while GOD has them sitting down in heaven. There is no evidence of God's anointing on their ministries or any of the works that are being done through their congregational members. On the contrary, their ministry is as dead men's bones. These are referred to in heaven as "the worldly church." They exalt one another in leadership based on the individual's educational level, natural ability to organize, natural ability to entertain, etc. They bring in well-known speakers who claim to be knowledgeable on how the gifts of the Holy Spirit are to function within the body when, in fact, they are only aware of and able to identify mere natural talents that individuals may possess. Yet they call them the gifts of the Spirit, but the <u>true</u> Spirit of God has little or nothing to do with any of it.

The same goes for office gifts as stated in I Corinthians 12:28: *"And <u>God</u> has appointed in the church, first apostles, second prophets, third teachers, then miracles, then gifts of healings, helps, administrations, various kinds of tongues."* When men choose men based on their <u>natural</u> qualifications, there is nothing happening in the supernatural.

We can break down this Scripture and see that each and every one of these office gifts was meant to function <u>through</u> the supernatural power of GOD. Miracles, gifts of healings, and diversity of tongues <u>cannot</u> operate apart from the supernatural power of GOD!

If the other office gifts named within this single passage of Scripture were not also designed to function by this same supernatural power of GOD, then we would be looking at serious unbalance. Yet, this is what we are seeing within the walls of too many denominational and non-denominational churches, whose staff claim to be teachers, administrators, or have the gift of hospitality.

Thus we have <u>self</u>-appointed teachers instructing their peers on the gifts of the Holy Spirit, such as speaking in tongues for example, when they have never spoken in tongues themselves. Who among us would consent to being instructed in how to play a piano by one who has never played the piano, even if he did refer to himself as a piano instructor? How futile would this be? Yet, this is what is transpiring within many churches all over America. The HOLY SPIRIT is being *quenched*, the HOLY SPIRIT is being *grieved*. and the Body of Christ is *oblivious!*

We, as born-again Christians, have been missing GOD on many levels. We have failed to recognize those whom GOD has been raising up all along. The Lord has shown me—throughout many years—that some of people's refusal to accept the Prophets and Seers, for example, has been for lack of applying themselves to sincere study and prayer. Some refusal is based on an unwillingness to admit one could be mistaken in how they have perceived these to operate. Some refusal to accept those who God has called to function in these capacities is rooted in pride. Some refusal is from the demonic strongholds of Jezebel—control, manipulation, and intimidation. Much adversity is from members being influenced by spirits of jealousy and competitive spirits who have no problem with others growing as long as they don't pass them by.

As believers we must <u>focus our eyes on the LORD</u> by **commanding** our spiritual eyes to open and our spiritual ears to unstop to hear what the SPIRIT OF THE LORD is saying to the Church. Could it be that He is searching for those who are willing to make up the hedge of protection around the Church and stand in the gap before Him? Could it be that He is searching for those who are willing to lay down their lives and take up their own cross to <u>follow Him</u> in the same capacity as did the early Church? Could it be that He is searching for men and women who desire to **really know Him?** What could we possibly have to hold on to that compares to the awesomeness of *knowing* GOD and experiencing His presence in our lives? Couldn't we choose to let go of the very things that are holding us back?

In Daniel 11:32, we are told that the people who **do know their God** shall be strong and do exploits! Example: In the life of Daniel (the Prophet) we can see that he was granted GODLY WISDOM with great skill and spiritual understanding into life and death matters. When King Nebuchadnezzar had a dream that escaped him afterward, he called for the wise men of his day to tell him what he dreamed and give him the interpretation of the dream. They all insisted that if he would tell them the dream, they would give him the interpretation. They told King Nebuchadnezzar there was no one who could tell him what he dreamed and insisted that no king, lord, or ruler would even request such a thing of them. This angered the king, and he ordered their execution—the death of all the "wise men"—including Daniel. However, Daniel went in to the king and asked for time to pray about it. Then the secret was revealed to Daniel in a night vision. He was able to give King Nebuchadnezzar the dream he had and also the interpretation. He was also careful to give Glory to GOD by explaining to the king that this information is not made available to the wise men, astrologers, magicians, or soothsayers, but <u>can only be revealed by GOD in heaven</u>! Daniel experienced God's presence in his life and ***knew*** God in ways most of us will never understand. Because of that relationship with the LORD he risked his life with confidence that God's plan would win the day!

Many years ago, after receiving the Baptism of the HOLY SPIRIT, I was praying for a young woman at our local *Women's Aglow* meeting. I had my hand on her shoulder as I was praying in the spirit. Several minutes passed as much of my prayer took the form of *praying in tongues*. Then it occurred to me to share with her how people in the Old Testament would seek out answers from the wise men of their day, astrologers, soothsayers, etc. As a last resort, they would turn to the prophets of GOD. I compared this to how we still do this today by seeking help and counsel through the worldly system, then again, as a last resort, we turn to JESUS.

Later that afternoon, she called me asking me if I spoke Spanish. I responded with a few words I knew in Spanish, but then told her those were all the words I knew.

"Well, the words you spoke to me *in tongues* this morning was in Spanish," she said.

"What was I saying?" I asked.

"The first words I heard were, ***'Diane, I love you,'*** and the rest of the message was the same thing you said to me in English afterward."

This was a modern-day <u>real-life example</u> of speaking in *tongues* <u>with</u> the interpretation *of tongues*. Yet, I was not even aware at the time that I was operating in the gift of tongues with interpretation of tongues. Diane went on to explain that her father was in the military stationed in Barcelona during her high school years, and that was when she learned the Spanish language.

> The Apostle Paul had much to say about this topic, and in I Corinthians 14:5-13 he wrote, *"Now I wish that you all spoke in tongues, but even more that you would prophesy; and greater is one who prophesies than one who speaks in tongues, unless he interprets, so that the church may receive edifying. But now, brethren, if I come to you speaking in tongues, what will I profit you unless I speak to you either by way of revelation or of knowledge or of prophecy or of teaching? Yet even lifeless things, either flute or harp, in producing a sound, if they do not produce a distinction in the tones, how will it be known what is played on the flute or on the harp? For if the bugle produces an indistinct sound, who will prepare himself for battle? So also you, unless you utter by the tongue speech that is clear, how will it be known what is spoken? For you will be speaking into the air. There are, perhaps, a great many kinds of languages in the world, and no kind is without meaning. If then I do not know the meaning of the language, I will be to the one who speaks a barbarian, and the one who speaks will be a barbarian to me. So also you, since you are zealous of spiritual gifts, seek to abound for*

the edification of the church. Therefore let one who speaks in a tongue pray that he may interpret."

Another incident that comes to my mind while delving into Daniel's experience—and seeing a correlation in the ways that the HOLY SPIRIT still deals with the Church today—happened shortly after I received the Baptism of the HOLY SPIRIT. While attending a series of Kathryn Kuhlman[2] healing services in Chicago, I was connected with a dynamic sister in the LORD who became my *spiritual mentor*. We spoke over the phone on a daily basis, and all our conversations were centered on Scriptures from the Word of God. There was so much to glean from this relationship that words would fail me should I attempt to relay how spiritually enriching it was. I marveled at the degree of wisdom and understanding that came from this *spiritually seasoned* woman of God—Nadyne.

One day Nadyne called to ask me to pray about something she felt God was speaking to her about. She was always putting me to the challenge, drilling me, testing me, and giving me new assignments. This proved to be another challenge because she wanted me to pray **to see** what GOD was saying to her and to get back with her on it! She might as well have been asking me to pray for the interpretation of a dream without telling me what she had dreamed. I had nothing to go on; no hints, no clues, just pray.

So I prayed asking the LORD to show me what He was showing her. I saw a vision of a flock of geese flying in formation. They were like cartoon characters with the goose in the lead turning its head around backwards to the rest of the flock. Words coming out of his

---

[2] Kathryn Kuhlman—leader in Pentecostalism in the world between 1940 and 1976.

mouth were, "Would one of you come up here and help me?" (This concept we can see in sporting events like cycling where drafting is involved. When a cyclist in the lead who has been working the hardest needs to rest, he will signal the group behind that he is *rolling off*.)

When I shared with Nadyne what the Lord had shown me with the vision of the flock of geese, she told me what the Lord was showing her. With Nadyne, it was not a vision, but in the natural. She had been trying to locate a certain star which had previously been positioned a distance off from the moon. She had not been able to see it anywhere, the reason being that the angle of visibility was now on the very tip of the moon. Instinctively, in her spirit, she was sensing GOD had a message in this for her. She required confirmation that needed to come from an unbiased *revelation* apart from any coaxing or helpful hints that would allow the enemy to steal it from her with thoughts of doubt that she had let me in on any part of what was being shown to her personally prior to her calling me.

What she was seeing along with what was shown to me are both addressed in I Corinthians 15:39-41…

> *"All flesh is not the same flesh, but there is one flesh of men, and another flesh of beasts, and another flesh of **birds**, and another of fish. There are also heavenly bodies and earthly bodies, but the glory of the heavenly is one, and the glory of the earthly is another. There is one glory of the sun, and another glory of the **moon**, and another glory of the **stars**, for **star** differs from **star** in glory."*

From this, Nadyne felt she was being shown that God was moving her into position of greater responsibility in her role as "intercessor." God's glory is seen through answered prayer!

When Nadyne prayed for me in her house, I could tell she was praying for me in my house. One example of this happened at 6:45 a.m. on a morning that I had agreed to take over the sponsoring of a bus trip to a Kathryn Kuhlman service in St. Louis. I woke up that morning feeling the anointing of the HOLY SPIRIT all over me. I asked my husband if he was sensing anything like *anointing*. He said he didn't sense anything happening although it would not have been unusual for him if he had.

A few hours later, as a large group of us was boarding the bus, here came Nadyne asking me if I had felt the HOLY SPIRIT anointing me <u>that morning</u>. I responded, "Yes! I did!" Hearing what was said, Gerald asked, "Wasn't that about 6:30?" Nadyne and I both replied at the same time, "No, it was quarter 'til 7!" When the Holy Spirit connects people for His Kingdom Purposes, the link is tri-fold: God (Father/Son/Holy Spirit) and the two (or more) people involved. God's Word, God's Glory, God's Purposes are always central.

Nadyne and her husband were attending one Baptist church in our city, and my husband and I were attending another Baptist church. Neither of these churches endorsed or recognized teachings about the Baptism of the HOLY SPIRIT and the church our family attended was *adamantly* against it. There were an increasing number of couples in our church, as well as a number of other churches within the city and suburbs outside the city, who were experiencing the Baptism of the Holy Spirit. Thus, more and more classrooms on Sunday mornings began to teach on each specific church's theology pertaining to the gifts of the HOLY SPIRIT.

Over a two-year period, we sat in classroom after classroom listening to erroneous teaching on this topic. What was being taught, generally speaking, was that *speaking in tongues* is not for today, healing is not for today, anointing with oil serves no purpose other than application for medicinal purposes, miracles are not for today, etc.

Even though it bothered me to hear all this, I was not saying anything. The few people who spoke out with boldness were called, "trouble makers." Not only did I not want to wear that label, I had avoided being confrontational. As teenagers, my twin sister and I would rather chance being reprimanded in the principal's office than to stand up in front of the class to give a book report. I also avoided speaking in front of any group. Some of these classrooms at church were made up of 30-50 people!

After a couple years of cowardly behavior in these Sunday school classrooms, I had a vision that jolted me out of my comfort zone. In the vision, I was standing in the center of the little country road in front of our house. I knew it was noontime with the sun shining brightly overhead when suddenly the day started turning to darkness. Dark clouds rolled in as I stood in wonderment at what was taking place in the sky overhead. Then all dark! Suddenly a hole broke in the darkness, and a very bright light came streaming through the hole right to where I was standing. I could feel the **presence of GOD** in this stream of light and as the light hit me with this *awesome* presence, I fell to the pavement on my knees with my forehead touching the asphalt.

Within that vision came another vision where I saw a giant ear in the sky! I was hearing words being spoken: *"This is your ear. It has been **dull of hearing, and you have run out of time.**"* I began to respond to the voice by begging GOD to give me one more chance. I was saying, "Please, please, just give me one more chance. I'll be obedient. I'll be obedient. Please, please, please just give me one more chance." I was still saying those words as the vision ended.

Needless to say, sudden change came into my life because that vision was so real. I was not going to take any chances. From the day of that vision and moving forward, I found boldness I didn't know I had!

With this newfound confidence and willingness to SPEAK UP, came persecution unlike anything I could have imagined! Our children were being persecuted, as well. We stayed in that church until the HOLY SPIRIT released us to go which came at the same time the congregation voted to terminate the pastor because he was being *too soft* on the *charismatics*!

Our own decision to leave at the same time came yet through another vision I had where I was watching my husband taking live fish out of a pond that had both live fish and dead fish. He was transporting the live fish to a new body of water and leaving the dead fish in the old pond. That water had become stagnate as our season there had ended and we were being led to move on.

Nearly a decade had passed after that when persecution took a different turn to a degree that there was no one I could talk to about it. By then, Nadyne and her husband had moved away to be close to their children in a different state and there was no pastor or close friend I had to turn to. In fact, this persecution involved my very closest friends. (Nevertheless, we need to continually remind ourselves that persecution comes from the rulers of darkness, <u>not</u> people. Yet the rulers of darkness will use people as instruments to carry out their assignments against the saints of God!)

Whether we realize it or not, the HOLY SPIRIT shows us things about situations to help us *outwit the enemy* even when we could construe it as coming through our own thoughts. In the midst of the persecution that had been coming against me from yet a different angle, I had a dream about a man who was coming to speak at one of our local churches. All I knew was his name, but I had no knowledge of who he was or where he had attended Bible College. As it turned out later, I discovered that he had been a student of one of the most powerful world-wide ministries in the country, one of which we had been financially supporting for years. In the dream, this man was encouraging me and GOD knew I needed to be encouraged! Encouragement can come through people, but not all *people encouragement* is ordained by GOD. This was one of those times when I couldn't chance receiving any word of encouragement without the assurance that GOD was in it.

I tried to get a baby-sitter for our three children, but I couldn't find one. My thoughts were to give up on going to listen to this speaker. But then if I didn't go, I would always wonder what he would have said to bring encouragement to me. On the other hand—because I saw him in a dream—what if I did manage to get there and he didn't say or do anything to encourage me? I would have never had faith in another dream after that as being from the LORD!

I decided to go and take our children with me. The pastor of the church spoke for an hour before he turned the meeting over to the speaker. All three children were sitting patiently in the pew beside me, and then the guest speaker got up to talk. Throughout his entire dissertation, nothing seemed to reach out at me to disquiet the fiery assaults that had been confronting me.

Sitting there, I remembered what a popular woman preacher on television had said, "When faced with a situation, we need to make things **easy on ourselves and hard on GOD!**" I knew I was in this kind of situation. So I had decided that I wasn't going to do <u>anything</u> to bring it about of my own volition. If this man was going to encourage me—like he was encouraging me in the dream—it was going to have to be from GOD! I was not going to go forward for prayer at the end of the service. I was not going to confront him in any way to indicate I was dealing with any major issues. (This is not meant to discourage anyone from going up for prayer that is being offered in any church service, prayer meeting, or any one-on-one opportunity for prayer. However, in my own situation at that particular season in my life, I felt it would serve me best not to.)

When the service ended, and all the people who went forward for prayer had been prayed over, I got up with my three children and headed out the front door. Then before the door could hit me on my way out, this guest speaker called after me!

"Wait a minute! Come back in here! Aren't you supposed to be talking to me?" He came and got us and brought us back into the sanctuary, sitting us down on the back pew. Then sitting down with us he said, "Now tell me what is going on with you."

I described my everyday walk with the LORD, then explained my situation and the accusations that were coming against me. Immediately, he said these words...

"First of all; your eyes are the windows to your soul, and there is nothing of that nature in your eyes." The walk I had been on with the Lord, as I described to him, went right in line with the teachings he had received that prepared him to expose enemy tactics that were being used against me. "Let me tell you what has been coming against you," he said. He then went into detail describing how those who are closest to me are not going to believe that I can hear from God <u>if they</u> do not. This is especially true in the area of dreams and visions. Their opinion will be that if God isn't speaking to <u>them</u> through dreams and visions, then God isn't going to speak to me through dreams or visions.

Not only were these attacks against me coming from the *rulers of darkness* over the region where we lived; but he also referred to the service that night, pointing out how these same satanic forces were carrying out assignments against him throughout the entire evening. Assignments which he understood had been quite obvious to me.

One way, however, the enemy got *outwitted* that night was in the fact that I held off going up for prayer. For had I tried to help GOD out in any way, the devil would have come back at me later trying to *reason* that none of this **encouragement** would have taken place had I not gone forward to initiate it in the first place. Over these many years, I have had numerous opportunities to remind myself of the very wise and timely *word of Wisdom* that came through that woman preacher on television. "Whenever we find ourselves in a tough situation, we are to **make it easy on ourselves and hard on GOD." He is always ready to bless us with what we need!**

> Ephesians 1:3 says, *"Blessed be the God and Father of our Lord Jesus Christ, who has blessed us with every spiritual blessing in the heavenly places in Christ."*

And Psalm 139:7-12, *"Where can I go from Your Spirit? Or where can I flee from Your presence? If I ascend to heaven, You are there; If I make my bed in Sheol, behold, You are there. If I take the wings of the dawn, if I dwell in the remotest part of the sea, even there Your hand will lead me, and Your right hand will lay hold of me. If I say, 'Surely the darkness will overwhelm me, and the light around me will be night,' even the darkness is not dark to You, and the night is as bright as the day. Darkness and light are alike to You."*

GOD is continually—through His HOLY SPIRIT—connecting people with people for His Kingdom Purposes. Throughout the Scriptures and in our everyday lives, we encounter **Divine connections** and **re-connections** taking place.

Periodically, as we were growing up, our mother would share stories with my sisters and me that revolved around her own life at that particular time. She and Dad met in business college, were married, and worked for nine years building their own business prior to starting a family. Even though many of their friends remained close to their grass roots, as did our parents; some did not. Several went on to compose music in New York and another to Chicago to study art.

One weekend when my husband and I went to a homecoming event in his home town, we drove past the home where one of these men used to live. As we drove past, I remarked out loud to Gerald that I would like to meet this man someday.

No sooner did we arrived at the park on the square where approximately 200 people had gathered at the pavilion, when my eyes zeroed in on one particular man seated on the other side of the pavilion. I was sitting next to my mother's cousin, Ruth. This man who had caught my eye was wearing a white shirt, turquoise jewelry, and I thought he resembled one of my uncles. I pointed him out to Ruth and asked her if she didn't think that man looked like Mother's brother—referring to him by his nickname. Ruth did agree with me that he resembled my uncle but went on to explain to me that this gentleman had a son who lived in the big house across from the grade school. <u>This was the man who I had just voiced, less than a half hour previously, I would like to meet someday</u>! For all I knew, or any of my family knew, he was still living in Chicago where he had spent his entire career working at the Illinois Art Institute. Now I was picking him out of a crowd of close to 200 people when I had no idea what he looked like, let alone any idea he had retired and recently moved back to the town he grew up in!

A team of wild horses could not have stopped me at that point from finding someone to introduce me to him. I ran and got my friend, Janice, who I wrote about in the beginning of this book, to see if she by any chance knew him? Of course she did! Really! So she took me over to meet him and when he heard me say I was Edrie's daughter, his mouth flew open in total surprise! Our conversation went quickly back to the days I had heard so much about in my earlier years, and this encounter marked one of my most cherished **heavenly-orchestrated** Divine appointments! I couldn't wait to stop by Mother's house to tell her about it, and it blessed her to hear of the things he had recalled in my conversation with him.

Each Has a Role to Play

Within a few days, I stopped by his house to give him a copy of a book I had just had published. God's plan of Salvation was now in his hands. A cousin of mine who had lunch with him later reported to me that he was asking her what <u>she believed</u> about God. I can't help but believe that if he had not at some point in his life received Salvation through Jesus Christ, surely our meeting and subsequent visit had started him thinking. By the time he'd spoken to my cousin, he must have been giving serious thought to the Gospel message. However, we were never given that assurance.

Charles and Frances Hunter[3] wrote a book that proved to be a best-selling book in Christian stores across the country. It is titled, <u>Angels on Assignment</u>, and is about the experiences of Pastor Roland Buck who was visited by the angels Michael and Gabriel in his home from time to time. During one of those encounters, the angels explained to him <u>the role</u> they played in getting people in front of the believers who they know are most apt to be sharing the Gospel with them. If that person does not reach them with the message, or if the message is not received at that time, the angels circle around and bring them back to that same person or lead them to someone else who will share the Gospel with them until that person is open and receptive to the message.

In I Corinthians 3:7-8, Paul writes, *"So then neither the one who plants nor the one who waters is*

---

[3] Charles and Frances Hunter: known for their passion for the Lord and His healing powers.

anything, but God who causes the growth. Now he who plants and he who waters are one; but each will receive his own reward according to his own labor."

A specific modern day illustration of this passage of Scripture comes to mind from the year 2003 after the baton had been passed on to me where our farm operation was concerned. I had contracted with a young, perhaps overly zealous, friend of our son's by the name of Bill to rent the land. I had been attempting to sow seeds pertaining to the Gospel into the heart of this young man while wondering if anything I had said was having any kind of impact on him. To the contrary, what I had noticed was how he had started pushing some folks around, even those who had farmed the farm previous to his arrival.

One morning as I was reading in one of Smith Wigglesworth's[4] books, I read where he quoted the Scripture from Luke 3:4, *"As it is written in the book of the words of Esaias the prophet, 'The voice of one crying in the wilderness, Make ready the way of the Lord, make his paths straight.'"* To this, he had reiterated, **"without treading on other people and exalting undo rights."**

I couldn't help but take this opportunity to call this young man up to the house, sit him down at the kitchen table, and read to him what Smith Wigglesworth had written in his book. Those few words seemed to hit home with him as the Spirit of the LORD began to convict him. By the time we walked back out of the house together, his head was hanging low.

Then, just as he split off from me to head back down to the barn, a white pick-up truck drove in. This man had been driving on

---

[4] Smith Wigglesworth: British Evangelist and Faith Healer in the early years of Pentecostalism.

Each Has a Role to Play

a county road to Springfield from a town approximately 25 miles away. Because he had recently started a power-washing business, he thought he would stop by and leave a couple of his new business cards. With two cards in my hand, I decided to run one of them down to Bill before I went back into the house.

At the same time this other man (also by the name of Bill) saw that I was walking down to the barn. Instead of driving on out as intended, he circled around to the barn driveway coming up to where I had just handed off one of his business cards. A little small talk pursued after he introduced himself along with some pertinent questions relating to the farm situation across the country. Then, as if out of the blue, he asked Bill point blank, **"Have you ever invited Jesus into your heart?"**

Bill's first inclination was that I had planned this encounter. "Wait a minute. Do you know her? Does she know you?" he questioned. Assuring Bill that he had no plans of even stopping by in the first place but just happened to see my house across the field as he was driving by a mile away, he needed not say any more. Bill was already realizing that this was not a man-planned encounter but a God-planned **Divine connection!** He was *so ready to pray*! Bill from Jacksonville had no knowledge of the conversation that had just transpired at the kitchen table. We were all crying in awe of the moment as the three of us held hands, and Bill Brown led our Bill in a Salvation prayer that no doubt was springing out of the conviction of the HOLY SPIRIT that took place just prior to his arrival.

Later on that day, Bill was sharing with me that he had been all stressed over the farm situation, but after he got back in the combine his thoughts turned to how all those intricate details of the last hour had come about. Suddenly a peace came over him and a **presence**

of the LORD that carried with it an unexplainable *"knowing"* that everything was going to be alright!

GOD will go to great lengths to reach us *right where we are.* Whereas God impressed upon me to point out a wrong-doing in Bill's life, it did not seem like the right timing for me to question him about receiving Jesus as his Savior. GOD had someone else in mind who He knew **would ask** this very important question.

A short time after that GOD **re-connected** Bill with a close friend of his father's. Everything in this man's life had taken on new meaning since the last time they had seen each other. He had been *Born-again*, Baptized in the HOLY SPIRIT, and was now active in ministry along with running his own new business that the LORD had supernaturally opened doors to! He and his wife were attending a **full-gospel church**, and Bill couldn't wait to go check their church out!

Personal Notes: The Church today is only living in a small percentage of what GOD has for us when we compare the Body of Christ now to the early Church and the gifts of the Spirit that operated through them. There is so much more for us to be operating in if we can move away from the normal practices observed in most congregations to what we can **SEE** as **ideal** according to the Scriptures. Prayerful personal study of God's Word will allow the Holy Spirit to show us how to be the best Ambassadors of Christ we can be. Everything we need has already been given to us through Jesus' restoration of our *lives*. It is OUR JOB to pull it into our lives through Faith.

Chapter Four

Putting Angels to Work

When I realized that several of my friends and acquaintances had previously resided in the same homes—at different times—I looked upon it as if it was almost like playing *musical-houses*. It was an experience we all came to appreciate as many blessings from God. The pieces of this testimony may seem a little hard to follow at first, yet I know God's *detail-work* will be apparent as I relay these events.

I had joined a Bible study at my friend Janice's home on Checkerberry Lane. This Janice is a mutual friend of mine and the Janice I mentioned in chapter one. A short time later, Janice sold her condo on Checkerberry and moved to a home on Brighton Road. A woman by the name of Linda had purchased my parents' former residence, moving there around the same time Janice had moved into the home on Brighton which happened to be a former home of Linda's.

Prior to these moves, my friend Beverly had called me asking for help to find a home for her son Rodney and his family. Rodney had moved here from Florida where he had been painting airplanes for a living. When he moved back to Springfield, he had started his own cleaning business. However, because these two occupations were unrelated, he was required to have 20% down payment if he was to purchase a home.

During the interim, he and his wife and children were staying with his sister and her family. Even though Rodney was advertising his new business every way he knew how, his phone was **not ringing!**

Being a born-again Christian, he knew the power of prayer and laying his concerns at Jesus' feet. When we call out to God, out of our place of despair, He hears us! Thus, he had taken his two little girls to a nearby park, sat down on a bench situated on a hillside, and prayed about their situation. He needed to see the Lord move for him in a supernatural way because not only had his business failed to launch, neither did he have 20% to put down on a house.

A few days later, as he and I set out to go house shopping with my stack of information sheets, I was quoting Scriptures to him between every house showing reminding him that he is the seed of Abraham through Christ Jesus, and the Blessing Pact (Covenant) that was Abraham's belongs to him also.

I quoted several Scriptures from Deuteronomy 28 (KJV) beginning with verse (3) three, *"You are blessed in the city and blessed in the field; blessed is your basket and your store. You are blessed coming in and blessed going out. The LORD shall cause your enemies to be smitten before your face; if they come out against you by one way, they will flee before you seven ways. The LORD shall make you plenteous in goods and in the fruit of your ground. The LORD shall open his good treasure unto you and bless the work of your hands. The LORD shall make you the head and not the tail; above and not beneath in the land that He gives to you."*

Then I spoke God's Word from Philippians 4:19, (KJV) *"But my God shall supply all your needs according to His riches in glory by Christ Jesus."*

Also, Jeremiah 29:10 (KJV) *"For I know the thoughts that I think toward you, saith the Lord, thoughts of peace, and not of evil, to give you an expected end."*

As I continued to send Scriptures into Rodney's situation as a means of demonstrating the importance of God's Word to him, I was also believing to see a supernatural demonstration from heaven on his behalf.

Rodney called me a day or so later because he wanted me to look at a "For Sale by Owner" home with him. I met him on the property and Bob, the man who was showing us the home, recognized my name because he had heard his mother speak of me. Not only was her name Dorcas from the Bible, a most unusual name, but she had a most unusual life story. Now we were about to see God move in a most unusual way to bring **resurrection life** into Rodney's circumstances!

That same night, I had a dream that we were back in the basement of that home with Dorcas's son, Bob, showing it to us like he had done that day. Then I heard these words being spoken aloud <u>*in the air*</u>, **"This house is for Rodney and nobody else!"** Yet, we still didn't know where the money was coming from for the down payment on the financing.

A few days later Rodney's phone rang. The caller had seen the online ad about his cleaning services and was looking for a company to clean an entire mall in a town 60 miles away. Even though Rodney really wasn't equipped yet to handle a job of that magnitude, he agreed to go. He decided to put his full trust in God to give him the strength, wisdom, and the wherewithal to complete the job with excellence.

Because **faith** is an _action word_, and God expects us to move out in faith, He doesn't put easy things in front of us. If what we had to face was something we could accomplish in our own natural strength, then we wouldn't need God—we could take care of it on our own. This is how we grow from **faith** to **faith** (Romans 1:17), moving continually forward into bigger and better things that are beyond our own natural ability to accomplish.

> Hebrews 11:6 (KJV) says, _"But without faith it is impossible to please Him, for he that cometh to God must believe that He is and that He is a rewarder of them that diligently seek Him."_

After Rodney agreed to do this job, I had a vision that I was kicking a football and Rodney was catching it. He was running toward the end zone with players from the opposite team coming against him. Rodney was running **through, over,** and **around** all these other players from the opposite team. I realized then the Holy Spirit was showing us that faith had transferred from me to Rodney, and he was **RUNNING WITH IT** to the goal line! I was immediately reminded of the Apostle Paul's words in Acts 14:8-10 (KJV)...

> "*At Lystra a man was sitting who had no strength in his feet, lame from his mother's womb, who had never walked. This man was listening to Paul as he spoke, who, when he had fixed his gaze on him and had <u>seen that he had faith</u> to be made well, said with a loud voice, "Stand upright on your feet." And he leaped up and began to walk.*"

This helped me understand the position Rodney was in—feeling as if he was "without strength" or the ability to accomplish "standing up" to the job before him. Even so, Rodney took action and moved forward **IN FAITH**. This was no time to let go **of his grip** on faith; he had to **run with it**!

The devil doesn't like it when he sees us running in faith. He will throw obstacles in our path, set up ambushes, try to get us to fear, send in thoughts of doubt and unbelief, and blindside us every way he can to try to stop us from focusing on the end result. He doesn't want us to have a testimony of the goodness of God, the peace of God, the mercy of God, the grace of God, or the favor of God. He doesn't faint just because he sees us pick up our Bibles. He doesn't get an instant headache the minute he sees us get out of bed in the morning. Don't we wish!

> The Apostle John reminds us of Jesus' words when He said, "*The thief comes only to steal and kill and destroy; I came that they may have life, and have it abundantly.*" (John 10:10)

> And in I Peter 5:8, Peter wrote, *"Be of sober spirit, be on the alert. Your adversary, the devil, prowls around like a roaring lion, seeking someone to devour."*

> II Corinthians 10:3-6, *"For though we walk in the flesh, we do not war according to the flesh, for the weapons of our warfare are not of the flesh, but divinely powerful for the destruction of fortresses. We are destroying speculations and every lofty thing raised up against the knowledge of God, and we are taking every thought captive to the obedience of Christ...."*

Rodney was well aware that he was fighting unseen enemy forces. We, too, need to recognize that we are in a **war!** In fact, we should be praying for new and refreshed heightened abilities to discern malicious spirits. We must ask the Holy Spirit to show us which Scriptures <u>to send</u> into each situation—the <u>specific Scriptures</u> that are designed to bring us into VICTORY. JESUS HAS ALREADY WON OUR VICTORY ON THE CROSS OF CALVARY! Now we must learn His ways of moving into that Victory.

> Hebrews 12:1-2, *"Therefore, since we have so great a cloud of witnesses surrounding us, let us also lay aside every encumbrance and the sin which so easily entangles us, and let us run with endurance the race that is set before us, fixing our eyes on Jesus, the Author and Perfecter of faith, Who for the joy set before Him*

endured the cross, despising the shame, and has sat down at the right hand of the throne of God."

The demons who are carrying out assignments from the rulers of darkness and powers and principalities of the air—the demons who work for Satan and do his bidding on the earth—they are the ones who hate God <u>and hate us</u>. When we war against these demons in the unseen realm <u>with</u> the **Word** of God and give praise and worship TO GOD, we are positioning ourselves to be the <u>overcomers</u> that the Scriptures have declared us to be.

I John 5:4, *"For whatever is born of God overcomes the world; and this is the victory that has overcome the world–our faith."*

And in Romans 8:37-39, *"But in all these things we overwhelmingly conquer through Him Who loved us. For I am convinced that neither death, nor life, nor angels, nor principalities, nor things present, nor things to come, nor powers, nor height, nor depth, nor any other created thing, will be able to separate us from the love of God, which is in Christ Jesus our Lord."*

Demon forces are very militant, regimented, organized, and strategic. Keeping in mind that the devil has been at this a whole lot longer than we have, we need to move into a higher dimension of prayer where we will experience a new level of understanding, faith, and knowledge. <u>We are destined to walk with God</u> and **take**

new territory that has been marked for KINGDOM PURPOSES according to His plans for us both individually and corporately.

The first thing that came against Rodney was made known to me when he called in **panic mode** to tell me he was on his way to his new job—<u>cleaning the mall</u>—and only <u>one</u> member of the crew he had lined up was able to go with him.

I told Rodney to PRAISE THE LORD all the way there! I don't know if he did, in fact, praise the Lord during every minute of the long drive or not. But I can pretty much guess that he was praising the Lord at least the biggest share of the time. When he arrived, he was able to sign on a new crew. He was seeing God provide everything that he needed to accomplish the task at hand—even in the way of supplies and equipment where he was falling short. One immediate solution was that there <u>just happened</u> to be contractors working on the site who had scaffolds or man-lifts. They loaned him their equipment so that he could get his men up to the windows that needed to be cleaned. Later, Rodney told me that **every time he needed something** he didn't have, he turned, and there was the solution.

At the end of the two weeks, he had finished the job and was able to net over and above the amount he needed for the 20% down payment required for his financing to be approved. Going on for the **touchdown**, so to speak, he was able to close on the For-Sale-by-Owner house and move his family in!

It wasn't until a year later when he was in his front yard talking to me on his cell phone that he looked across the street and came to the realization that the home he and his family ended up in was <u>across the street</u> from where he had gone with his little girls that day to pray about his house situation. The bench they

were sitting on was positioned catty-cornered on a hillside in the park facing their new home.

As perfect as that house was, and as happy as they were to be there, before the second year ended Rodney received a notice from the zoning board. Even though it was okay for him to operate his business from his home, he was only allowed to park <u>one work vehicle</u> in the driveway at any one time. By then, God had blessed him with several work vans. So what was he to do this time?

He called me and told me his predicament. My first thought was that he needed to find a building nearby where he could park his vans; a place close enough so that he could walk there or drive there. However, when I went onto the computer to see if there was anything close to the description of what he needed, I found a home which was actually <u>outside the city limits.</u> This house was a tri-level cedar home, multiple roof levels, and very contemporary. It had 3700 square feet of living space with four bedrooms, three bathrooms, and attached 2-car garage. It probably had $25,000 worth of concrete drive with curbs and most likely another $25,000 in beautiful landscaping on an acre and a half lot. However, this home was over twice the price that he paid for the first house just two years earlier. Once again he needed to see the hand of God at work in his life if this was where God wanted him to relocate.

One of the things that he thought would help to get him over there was if he could sell the first home without having to pay a real estate commission. Ordinarily, when you are in a contract to purchase a property that is contingent upon the sale of your own home, the Realtor representing the seller will insist that you place your home on the market with a real estate agent as soon as possible. They don't want to wait for a seller to try to bring in his own buyer in a situation when **time is of the essence.** Yet, in this case, there was really no time to place his home on the market anyway.

I held an open house on the south end of town in a 2-story duplex when this little lady walked in and told me the name of the company she worked for on the north side of town. She went on to say she wanted to buy on the <u>north</u> end, **preferably around the park.**

There was Rodney's house just sitting there **across from the park** waiting for the buyer to come along. I gave her his name and phone number, and she bought the home directly from him. I didn't get paid a commission on the sale of his home, but I did get paid a commission on the home he moved into. **The fact that God literally dropped the buyer of Rodney's home into our laps made it possible for *three* deals to close in a timely fashion** as you consider that the seller of the home Rodney was buying had also purchased a home that he needed to move into right away.

That seller's name was Rick, and he had <u>purchased</u> the home he sold to **Rodney** from **Linda** who had moved to the house on Brighton Road that **Janice** purchased several years later when she moved from her condo on Checkerberry Lane! **Now you, too, can see the *musical-house* miracles that God orchestrated.**

Even though I referred to Linda as an acquaintance at the time this was all going on, we have become close friends over the years! Ten years after purchasing my parents' home, Linda moved to Florida and I have had the opportunity to stay with her there in a lovely condominium that overlooks the Caloosahatchee River!

Another benefit to God's detailed plans in the midst of these circumstances was that more women were being added to Janice's Bible study **because of the miracles that had transpired!** Not only did Rodney's mother join the Bible study, but her sister and another friend along with the young woman who had purchased Rodney's home across from the park.

Then My Own Move.

Little did I realize then, but it wasn't too much longer before the Lord moved me from my country home into the city, just up the street from Rodney's family. Prior to this time, I was in the habit of claiming from Scripture that <u>my steps are ordered of the Lord</u>.

> **"The steps of a man are established by the LORD, and He delights in his way."** Psalm 37:23

I had lived on our family farm since 1976 and was perfectly content living there. Our son, Jason, and his wife, Bridget, had been hinting that they would like to raise their boys on the farm. Even though I had been mowing acres of grass in the summer, shoveling snow in the winter, and caring for a home that was too large for me, I wasn't taking the hint.

One day they decided to look themselves for a home in or near Springfield, and they went on the computer to find some homes for me to show them. The first home was totally out of the question with way too much work needing to be done. After viewing the 2nd home, however, we were all in agreement that it was more to <u>my</u> own liking. This home had everything that I would have listed as special features if I had made up a list for myself—which I hadn't done or even thought to do. Subsequently, I ended up writing an offer on the home.

Prior to our viewing it, the home had sold to a couple contingent upon their home selling. That meant I had a 72-hour waiting period after the sellers accepted my offer in order to give the first buyers an opportunity to get their home sold during which time they held their own open house. Time was also of the essence for this sweet Christian couple, who I had presented my offer to, because they had plans to leave for the Philippines where they were going to be serving a two-year missionary assignment.

At some point within those next three days, I had a vision as I was waking up one morning. In the vision, I saw myself opening the back door of this new home to my children as they were coming in. I was asking them, "How do you like me in this house?" I woke up from the vision thinking, "**LORD, you are moving me into that house!**" I knew that was the Holy Spirit's way of letting me know (prior to my hearing from the owners) that God was, indeed, moving me to the city.

Jason and Bridget immediately put their present home on the market, I began to pack, and the couple I purchased my new home from went on to spend two sacrificial—yet blessed—years on the mission field.

Now Off To China!

Not only did God bless me with this home in the city, but the Lord continued to bless me and my family in various other ways. I had turned on television one afternoon when Marilyn Hickey[5] (Evangelist and Bible Teacher) was interviewing Joan Hunter[6]. Joan is the daughter of Charles and Francis Hunter, who were not only close friends of Marilyn's, but renowned ministers of healing themselves and well-known among leadership in the Charismatic Renewal, as is

---

[5] Marilyn Hickey: International speaker and teacher of the Bible and on healing.
[6] Joan Hunter: Minister, dynamic teacher, author, and anointed healing evangelist.

Marilyn. Now Joan has picked up the mantel and has been following in her parents' footsteps to carry God's healing anointing forward.

It was during the break when an upcoming missions/ministry trip to China was being announced, and chills were going all over me non-stop. Was this some kind of witness of the Spirit that I was to go on this trip? I wondered?

The first thing I did was to call my daughters and run this idea past them. Of course, they were excited to think there might be a possibility of us going to **China!** Then I did some figuring in my check book and ruled the entire idea out. I called my girls back to say, "China's off. No way."

To those of you who find yourselves reading this chapter right now, let me ask you a question. How many *dreams* and *aspirations* have you let slip by because you couldn't see your way to first base, let alone imagine the possibility of seeing those ambitions come to full fruition in your lives?

Not only have we allowed the enemy of our souls to rob us of the blessings that God has had in His mind for us throughout our lifetimes, but we have also robbed ourselves by listening to our own thoughts—*thinking* that was derived from natural human logic.

Within a day or so of ruling out the possibility of going to China, I woke up in the morning with a vision (as if waking up from a dream) of myself lying on the ground at night. I could see **stars in the sky above me, trees around me, and the thought in my head was, "This feels like China ground underneath me!** My natural logic was being messed with big time. Praise the Lord!

Later that day when I went onto my favorite prophetic website (*The Elijah List*[7]), there was an article by Prophet Kim Clement[8]. Kim was sharing with his readers how God had told him He couldn't get His Church to believe for the REDEMPTION of **billions of souls!** (This WAKE UP CALL to the churches continues to be repeatedly shouted by respected Prophets around the world.)

Kim asked God, "Why are You telling me this?" Kim was being shown countries in the Far East like China, Japan, and Korea and God was telling him that He wanted him to prophesy—**prophesy to the sky and to the trees and to the earth!** He named the same three things that I was seeing in the vision when I woke up that morning!

Further down in the article, Kim quoted God again where God had said, "DON'T WORRY ABOUT THE MONEY." Well, I needed to hear that too because, even though I had the funds available to me for the trip, the concern that was tugging at my natural logic was how would I stretch the remainder of finances upon my return back home?

When I read Kim Clement's article I knew those elements confirmed my initial desire to GO to China with the *Marilyn Hickey Ministry* group. Over many years, as I study and grow in my personal relationship with the LORD, I have endeavored to develop a sensitivity to the *voice of the Holy Spirit* as it compares to the Scriptures and how the early church stayed in tune and in touch with **the Holy Spirit.**

I Corinthians 14 offers the main guidelines I try to follow as the Apostle Paul, under the inspiration of the Holy Spirit, wrote for us: (1) God does speak supernaturally through one person to another person

---

[7] The Elijah List: Daily prophetic writings from the Lord, regarding the days in which we live.
[8] Kim Clement: Delivers uplifting, prophetic words to heal the wounded.

or multiple people; (2) this *prophecy* speaks edification (building up), exhortation (encouragement) and comfort (consolation) to people; (3) what is spoken is mainly positive, however, when a warning comes it is meant to bring about a positive result.

Following the above confirmation—that my own vision gave me accurate guidance—I was reading in Isaiah 44 and came across verse 23 (KJV)

> *"Sing, O ye heavens; for the LORD hath done it: shout, ye lower parts of the earth: break forth into singing, ye mountains, O forest, and every tree therein: for the LORD hath redeemed Jacob, and glorified himself in Israel."*

I heard the Holy Spirit say that night, "There's a second Scripture." I read on further the next day and came to this Scripture in Isaiah 45:8 (KJV)

> *"Drop down, ye heavens, from above, and let the skies pour down righteousness: let the earth open, and let them bring forth salvation, and let righteousness spring up together; I the LORD have created it."*

Knowing now that I was being led by the Holy Spirit to go to China, **I was in *expectancy mode*** as to what KINGDOM PURPOSE was in store for us on this trip which I immediately signed up for.

My friend, Janice, who I made mention of in the beginning of this chapter, shared with me how the Lord had made it possible for her to accompany the *Marilyn Hickey Ministry* team on a trip to China and the Philippines in February of 1987. Janice was reading in a MHM monthly magazine about the trip. She had never had a desire to travel to Asia, but this time she had a **burning desire to go!**

Because she knew the Lord wanted her to go, she called the trip coordinator even though it was past the due date to sign up for the trip. She was told that she could go, but it was three weeks before departure and she was <u>without the money and without a passport</u>. She was teaching school and not sure she could get permission to leave. Quite unexpectedly, her mother-in-law gifted her and her husband with some money! The schoolboard gave her two days leave (unpaid). There were two weekends in the trip, and the last day of the trip was on a school holiday. The schoolboard never did dock her for the two days as they said they would, and her passport came the day before they left. <u>She had received her passport in less than three weeks when it generally took six weeks at that time</u>.

They went to Hong Kong first, smuggled Bibles into Hong Kong, and then went to the Philippines and ministered with *Praise Fellowship Church*. They went house to house and people said, "Yes", they wanted to know Jesus, and then they prayed for them to receive the Baptism of the Holy Spirit! Lester Sumrall's nephew was the pastor of the church. They went out in the countryside to dedicate the wells that MHM had purchased, and when Marilyn Hickey preached an elderly village woman came forward and her sight was returned to normal!

Janice's testimony was such a great encouragement to me because everything she related to me from when she went in 1987 was **stirring my own faith that God would provide what was needed every step of the way for us.** We were facing some of the same issues where passports were concerned because I didn't have a passport yet, and one of my girls had an expired passport with the same limited amount of time to get prepared as Janice had. We welcomed the fact that Marilyn's trip coordinator, Marion Williams, was taking care of the passport issue along with many other things. She handed our passports to us upon arrival at the China Southern ticket counter!

Through Marion, I was also connected to the **editor for this book.** I had only recently begun to write these pages even though quite some time had passed since I first heard the Lord speak to me about it. The trip was no less than **dynamic** with God **showing up** from beginning to end. Marilyn is such a woman of Faith that she does not take NO for an answer when problems or issues arise. She prays about everything and expects God's results!

We arrived in Guangzhou, China, and flew from there to Chongqing where we were to board a cruise ship on the Yangtze River, but we were being told the water level was too low to board the ship where initially planned. Instead, we were going to have to go on buses along the river from town to town to town. I don't recall how many towns they told us we would be traveling through, three or four at least, before we would be where the water level was high enough to get the ship into the dock. That night during our prayer service, Marilyn prayed that **the river would rise overnight.**

I think it rained throughout the entire night, and we woke up the next morning being notified by the authorities that <u>the river rose so much overnight</u> we would be boarding the ship where originally planned! I remember one young man in particular who was **ecstatic** because he had never heard of that happening <u>ever before</u> in all of his life.

We held services in four different international churches where we were divided at times into groups after Marilyn preached. She taught mainly from the book of Daniel. Interpreters were assigned to the groups in order for us to understand the prayer needs of the people and assure their ability to understand what we were praying. When we returned home, we all had **renewed hearts for the Chinese people!**

Not long after returning home and contacting Royalene, with a request for her to pray about editing my work, I began reading two books she had recommended—samples of the work she had edited for Prophetess Mary Johnson-Gordon[9]. I was just into Mary's second book, *INSIGHTS, God's Use of Earthly Inhabitants for His Kingdom Purposes,* when I read, "**AGAIN, in reflection and insight,** I ask you, Dear Reader: To whom are you sent? To the great multitudes? To the lepers? Or to the one person who has the attention of God's heart?"

I then laid my head back to rest and immediately found myself in this vision where I was looking at a vertical wooden beam that appeared to be a beam from the Cross of Christ! There was a nail that had been hammered into one side of the beam diagonally with chains hung over the nail. Attached to each chain was a metal plate and they appeared very similar to dog tags that soldiers wear. There were different names of <u>countries</u> embossed on each metal plate and someone standing there handing them out as if each carried an assignment. I understood this person to be an angel, who was lifting each one separately off the nail and handing them over to the people who were standing there—waiting. One was being handed to me, and I saw that it had **"CHINA"** engraved on it! This angel-being, who looked like a man, whether man or angel I don't know which, said,

---

[9] Mary Johnson-Gordon: End Time Prophet, Preacher/Teacher, developing and instructing God's People for deeper *dimensions of service.*

"You can have this one." Then I was given instructions to pray for **liberty over the Chinese people!"**

That was the end of the vision, and I went back to find the place where I had left off reading in Mary's book. "To whom are you sent? To the great multitudes? To the lepers? Or to the one person who has the attention of God's heart?" Suddenly, I could see the correlation between the question she had asked in her book and the vision I was being shown right after I read it! I was also able to gain a sense of the **powerful anointing** that God has on Mary's work!

Each of the testimonies shared with you here are witness to HOW GOD LOVES US, gives us His attention, sends His angels to protect, and works with us in circumstances beyond our control. May God bless you with *understanding* hearts to comprehend ALL that He has for you.

Recent Events in Rodney's Life

Several months before finalizing this book, Rodney gave me his written permission to include his testimony in this chapter. However, he also asked me to include facts about the hard times he is once again facing. Rodney has experienced ill health over ten years after the testimony recorded herein above, and is again without work with no apparent job opportunities in sight. He has been unable to pay public service utilities; heat was cut off in their home and water disconnected plus a myriad of other misfortunes. As can be imagined, Rodney's faith and trust in God is wavering.

When Rodney asked me to add his "current life circumstances" to this book, I began to pray for him, his family, and their situation. I must admit that for a time I felt myself being pulled into the trap of worry and fears. However, the LORD has given me years of my own personal experiences to <u>know</u> that He is present with us even in the midst of ugly situations. So it is that I refuse to worry about their future. Instead, I am speaking God's Word into their lives once again. Proverbs 18:21 tells us that death and life are in the power of the tongue.

> *"And He [Jesus] said to His disciples, 'For this reason I say to you, do not worry about your life, as to what you will eat; nor for your body, as to what you will put on. For life is more than food, and the body more than clothing. Consider the ravens, for they neither sow nor reap; they have no storeroom nor barn, and yet God feeds them; how much more valuable you are than the birds!'"*
>
> (Luke 12:22-24)

On a recent television broadcast, it was reported that similar-type scenarios to Rodney's situation are playing out in epidemic stages across the country. We are reminded in II Corinthians 10:5 that we are destroying wrong thinking as we take thoughts captive to the obedience of Christ. If we give mental assent to what the enemy is bringing against us in this natural realm, we are coming into agreement with the very plans that his forces are waging against us. If we give those thoughts *words*, we are giving him consent to continue with his destructive endeavors. If we put these thoughts and words into writing, we are taking the schemes of the enemy yet another step further when instead we need to be calling those things that be <u>not as though they are</u>. Hebrews 4:17 tells us that God gives life to the dead and <u>calls into being that which does not exist</u>. We, being ambassadors of the Kingdom of God, are to also be imitators of God!

We must remember that in this world we will always be lured to worry and fret about something. We live on a fallen, fractured planet that is not as the LORD intended. The enormity of the life challenges we face can—and sometimes do—blind us. The best defense we have against the enemy of our eternal lives is to take all our cares to the Lord in prayer. When we do so and stand strong on God's promises to us, the enemy <u>must</u> flee because he can't stand to be in the Presence of God for very long. When we feel ourselves weakened, we must never forget to call upon our brothers and sisters in Faith to pray with and for us. Together we will keep the *prowling lions*—who want to kill, steal and destroy—at bay!

The challenges of this world give us MORE reason to sing praise songs to God, songs like **Jehovah Jireh** sung by Don Moen, for example. The lyrics honor God's Love and Mercy toward us on a daily basis and remind us that HIS GRACE IS SUFFICIENT to meet all our needs even as He gives His angels charge over us.

<u>Personal Notes:</u> Demonic forces consist of legions of spirits that are carrying out assignments against mankind. They are not wimps as some would like to portray them to be, neither is the devil himself to be compared to a toothless lion when it comes to knowing who the enemy is that we are up against. Sooner or later, we will find ourselves in situations where we are going to have to know how to war in the spirit and <u>it might as well be sooner</u>. Otherwise, we might find ourselves in a situation trying to nail up the shutters after the hurricane has already hit! Not good!

Chapter Five

The Spirit Makes Intercession

When the Apostle Paul wrote to his friends in Rome, he explained to them that the HOLY SPIRIT helps us in our infirmities. When we allow the HOLY SPIRIT to pray *through us* He is searching the will of GOD for us in a depth that we, in and of ourselves, are not able to comprehend. One of His active roles within the Trinity is to intercede through *groanings* that our human understanding is not able to tap into. We may be inspired to participate in this process by speaking aloud "in unknown tongues," or we may not be aware of the Holy Spirit's *groanings* on our behalf at all. However, we **are** being <u>helped</u> and <u>assisted</u> in taking hold of truths that are passed on to us through this process of *supernatural revelation* because it is God's desire that all things in our lives work together for our good and GOD's glory.

Paul wanted them to know that when he prayed in an *unknown tongue*, he was allowing this HOLY SPIRIT inspired intercession on his behalf to be engaged—be activated—even though his own understanding of what was being spoken was unintelligible to himself. In other words, he had no natural comprehension of this dialogue. And yet, not only did Paul *pray* <u>with</u> the Spirit, he then prayed in his own understanding. Paul also *sang* <u>with</u> the Spirit, and he sang with his own understanding. He would do one and then the other. What he allowed the HOLY SPIRIT to pray *through* him was a mystery to Paul, but it was not a mystery to GOD or to the HOLY SPIRIT.

> Paul stated in I Corinthians 14:2, *"For one who speaks in a tongue does not speak to men but to God; for no one understands, but in his spirit he speaks mysteries."*

Paul clearly says here that he who speaks in an unknown tongue speaks NOT to men, but to GOD. This was what was taking place on the Day of Pentecost when <u>men from every nation</u> heard the believers speaking in languages from the countries they, themselves, had come from. They heard them in these various languages PRAISING AND MAGNIFYING GOD for His wondrous works! This phenomenon was being witnessed by Jews living in Jerusalem who questioned how these Galileans were praising God with languages from the countries in which they, themselves, <u>were born</u>. We might compare this to America where we have one common language which is English. Yet, at the same time, there are people in America who speak various languages from the countries they came from, countries they <u>were born in</u>.

Because of the fact that they shared a common language, the Apostle Peter was able to stand up in their midst and give an account of what they witnessed. Peter, in so many words, was saying, "Listen up and give heed! These men are not drunk as you are supposing for it is only the third hour of the day! What you are witnessing is what was spoken of by the prophet Joel!" (Joel 2:28)

When Jesus departed, returning to His Heavenly Father after 40 days of walking the earth with His followers, He commanded them to wait for the promise of the Father, namely the Baptism of the HOLY SPIRIT as set forth in the first Chapter of Acts. Now we are hearing Peter in the second Chapter of Acts reiterating to them that <u>this</u> is the fulfillment of that promise—**<u>this</u>** which you are standing here seeing and hearing. This promise was not only for that moment of time, but was what they could expect to see and hear about in the future <u>until the Lord's return</u>.

Not only did Jesus command His disciples to wait for this mighty Baptism of the HOLY SPIRIT, we now understand that **this event would launch them into their future ministry.** Jesus also assured them that they would receive power to minister the Gospel throughout the then known world by way of this mighty Baptism of the HOLY SPIRIT. Then, last but not least by any measure, He instructed them to NOT go out without it!

> Acts 1:4-5: *"Gathering them together, He commanded them not to leave Jerusalem, but to wait for what the Father had promised, 'Which,' He said, 'You heard of from me; for John Baptized with water, but you will be Baptized with the Holy Spirit not many days from now.'"*
>
> Luke 24:49: *"And behold, I am sending forth the promise of My Father upon You; but you are to*

stay in the city until you are clothed with power from on high."

John 14:26: *"But the Helper, the Holy Spirit, whom the Father will send in my name, He will teach you all things, and bring to your remembrance all that I said to you."*

John 15:26: *"When the Helper comes, whom I will send to you from the Father, that is the Spirit of truth who proceeds from the Father, He will testify of me."*

Would Jesus require any less of you or me? Couldn't we conclude that if the early Church needed to be empowered by the HOLY SPIRIT in order to <u>do</u> exploits for GOD's Kingdom purposes, that we are also in just as much need to be empowered by the HOLY SPIRIT in order to reach our world today?

Not only do we have **need** to be empowered in the same manner the early believers were empowered to spread the Gospel to others, but we also need to be empowered to stay strong within ourselves, spirit, soul, and body. In Jude's letter of warning to the Church, regarding gross immorality and ungodliness, he admonished them to <u>contend earnestly for the faith</u> which was once and for all handed down to the saints. In verses 20 and 21 of Jude's letter, he writes,

"But you, beloved, BUILDING YOURSELVES UP ON YOUR MOST HOLY FAITH, praying in the HOLY SPIRIT, keep yourselves in the love of God, waiting

anxiously for the mercy of our Lord Jesus Christ <u>to eternal life</u>."

We can't give out what we don't have within us to give, and the devil would like it if we would all just lie down.
- The gift of the Holy Spirit is a *promised gift* to us.
- The Holy Spirit *empowers* us with Truth beyond the limits of our knowledge.
- The Holy Spirit *inspires* us in ways to communicate Truth to others.

In late February of 2011, I was awakened in the middle of the night with heart attack symptoms. Because we *know not how to pray as we ought*, the HOLY SPIRIT was right there with me to give instruction as to how I should pray. The first thing He said was, "Call the attack NULL AND VOID," which I did. Yet the symptoms persisted with tightness across my chest, up into my neck, and into my jaws and tongue. I remained totally reliant on the HOLY SPIRIT to help me get through this with Scripture after Scripture He gave me to send out against the enemy.

When we are praying in the Spirit, we are being shown things in the spirit realm that relate to the battle we are engaging in and the progress that is being made concerning the issues at hand. I prayed through until I was being shown that I had the victory. From that moment forward, I praised the LORD for that victory even though the symptoms did not subside until a while later.

True faith is when we can get to a place of seeing our desire accomplished in our spirits prior to seeing the manifestation in this natural realm. The world sees and then believes; but **we, as faith people, must first believe, then speak and see**. This concept was demonstrated throughout Jesus' ministry and in the lives of early Church believers.

> I Corinthians 4:13, *"But having the same spirit of faith, according to what is written, 'I BELIEVED, THEREFORE I SPOKE,' we also believe, therefore we also speak….."*

Billy Graham[10] shared that, as a young student studying at Florida Bible Institute in 1937, he would paddle across the river to a little island and **practice his preaching** to "all creatures great and small, from alligators to birds. If they would not stop to listen, there was always a congregation of cypress stumps that could neither slither nor fly away."

Mark Chironna[11] shared at one time on *Trinity Broadcasting Network*[12] that he had quit his job to go into the ministry. He had a family to support, but he wasn't getting any calls to preach. <u>Then the Holy Spirit told him to "hear the phone ring."</u> In other words,

---

[10] Billy Graham: Following Jesus as His Evangelist and Preacher to the world.
[11] Mark Chironna: Passionate preacher of the Gospel of Christ teaching that the wholeness of the Gospel leads to the experience of wholeness in our life.
[12] Trinity Broadcast Network (TBN): world's largest religious television network sharing the Gospel Message.

imagine you are hearing the phone ring. That was when he began to receive invitations to come preach.

As we learn to listen to GOD through praying in the Spirit, our spirit can connect with Divine instructions and Divine revelations. We may also be shown in the spirit realm the things that are being delivered to us prior to them becoming reality in this realm.

Shortly after those initial heart attack symptoms I experienced in the night, my friend, Linda (who had moved to Florida), came to visit me and ended up in the hospital with a pulmonary edema. While in the emergency room with Linda, those same symptoms I had experienced earlier came on me again. My daughter-in-law's mother happened to be on duty in the emergency room that night, and she insisted that I have an EKG done. The results were negative. NOTHING appeared to be wrong with my heart.

The next day, along with a mutual friend of ours, I returned to the hospital to visit Linda again. The same symptoms were coming on me the third time. Neither of the two attacks in the hospital lasted as long as the first one I experienced in the night.

After Linda was released from the hospital and left to go back to her home in Florida, I decided to follow up with my personal doctor to see what was going on with me. None of the tests I went through turned out good, especially the stress test I was given with a nuclear dye. Within a couple minutes after the injection, I experienced all the same symptoms over again and couldn't wait until the dye got back out of my system. This was a time when I needed to **engage** in spiritual warfare as never before!

When engaging in spiritual warfare, I needed to be in the Word of God for fresh manna. No soldier goes into battle on yesterday's meal. I could not be strengthened as I needed to be with nothing inside of me but left-overs. I needed to give the HOLY SPIRIT something to work with so I knew it was time to delve deeper into the Scriptures.

When the attack came against me in the beginning, I did not get out of bed and start reading my Bible! I was drinking waters from a reservoir of Scripture Truths I had already stored up. If we wait until something like this comes against us before we get into the Word of God, how will we be empowered enough to ward off such an enemy assault? Now I had to rebuild my arsenal if I was to turn the tables on the devil. In the heat of the battle, we need to look at the Cross, grab hold of what Jesus accomplished for us there, and place ourselves at the foot of the Cross **positioned to receive what we need by faith** through **praise and thanksgiving**! <u>We must have a revelation of this same Gospel the Apostles preached</u>! One of the first Scriptural passages the Holy Spirit led me to was when David said to Saul in I Samuel 17:32-37…

> *"'Let no man's heart fail on account of him; your servant will go and fight with this Philistine.' Saul said back to David, 'You are not able to go against this Philistine to fight with him; for you are but a youth while he has been a warrior from his youth.' But David said to Saul, 'Your servant was tending his father's sheep. When a lion and a bear came and took a lamb from the flock, I went out after him and attacked him, and rescued it from his mouth; and when he rose up against me, I seized him by his beard and struck him and killed him. Your servant has killed both the lion and the bear; and this uncircumcised Philistine will be like one of them, since he has taunted the armies*

The Spirit Makes Intercession

of the living God.' And David said, 'The Lord who delivered me from the paw of the lion and from the paw of the bear, He will deliver me from the hand of this Philistine.' And Saul said to David, 'Go, and may the Lord be with you.'"

I began to <u>pull</u> this story about David into my own situation because I felt I was up against a giant in my own life. Then the HOLY SPIRIT said to my spirit, *"Tell the doctors and the nurses."*

I sensed in my spirit when I heard this instruction that I was to tell the doctors and nurses about the miracles from God that I had seen Him do for me and my family in the past <u>just like David</u> did when he went back to what God had done for him in the past and boldly declared it to Saul. David decreed the works of the Lord so that Saul and all those assembled would know to give God glory for the victory he was about to win over Goliath! Instead of focusing on the size of the giant, David focused on the size of his God!

My next appointment was with the cardiologist who confirmed to me the results of the nuclear dye stress test and advised me that we needed to set up an appointment (over the next day or two at the most) for a heart catheterization. One of my daughters was with me, and we were seated in front of the doctor's desk in his private office. That made it easier for me to open up with him about what I was just about to tell him.

So I commenced with my dissertation about many of the miracles, especially those along the line of physical healing that we had already seen God do for us over past years. I started sharing with the doctor how the Lord had healed my other daughter of an allergy to gluten. She hadn't been able to eat anything with flour in it—which was about every edible product available at the time—and it only took one cookie to set it off. She would get huge hives all over her body with terrible itching that was almost unbearable, especially for a five-year-old.

One day they gave her a cookie at Sunday school, and that was all it took to send her into a rage all the way home from church. After we arrived back home, I had a little talk with Jesus! Then as I sensed **faith rising up inside of me** I went in and laid my hands on her, rebuking the allergy in the name of Jesus! As I continued to pray in the spirit, all the itching stopped! Within ten minutes, we could not find a welt on her body anywhere! Not only did God heal her of the allergy attack, He healed her of the allergy! Praise the Lord! Suzanne is now in her forties and has **never** had another allergic reaction to wheat flour.

I went on to tell him how I had scoliosis in my spine since my teen years, and one leg was ¾ inch shorter than the other leg. Eight years after I was married, a young 19 year-old Pentecostal boy came to our town from New York and prayed for me. My leg grew out instantly! My eyes were closed but I felt it growing; it grew and then stopped. When he said, "Just a little bit more," it grew again. My husband's eyes were open, and he could see it as it lengthened supernaturally. My back straightened out after that and has been in perfect alignment ever since.

I told him about our own dad who had a stroke and ended up in the hospital. After we prayed for him, tests showed no blockages, no narrowing in his arteries, and no coronary artery disease. He was in his late seventies at the time, and he walked out of the hospital as if he had never had a stroke! I was giving God all the glory!

When I got through sharing these testimonies with this cardiologist, my daughter Brenda said, "She can tell you a whole lot more stories than these!" The cardiologist began to question me about my beliefs—my Faith—and we talked quite a while longer.

Because he needed to synchronize his schedule with the stent specialist should a blockage be found, it ended up being scheduled a week later as opposed to the next day or so as originally intended. That gave me time to either stew about it or get back into spiritual warfare. I called a number of my Christian sisters to pray for me and—as the Holy Spirit led me to recall specific Bible events—I started putting myself into each and every one of them.

First, I imagined I was with the disciples when they were in a ship and the wind came against them in Mark 6:46-51. Jesus came walking on the water and almost passed them by. They didn't know who He was—even thought He might be a ghost—and they cried out in fear. That was the moment when Jesus said to them, *"Take courage; it is I, do not be afraid."* Then He got into the boat with them, and the wind ceased.

I put myself in the story where Paul and 276[13] men were in a ship during a violent storm (Acts 27:1-44), and they <u>all</u> escaped safe to land.

I thought of myself among the multitudes who were <u>all</u> healed, each and every one of them, time after time as Jesus and His disciples traveled the countryside for three years! Would Jesus heal them—every one—and leave me sick if I had been one of those who made up those multitudes of people?

---

[13] http://www.bible-history.com/past/pauls_ship_to_malta.html

II Corinthians 1:18-20 (KJV), it is written, *"But as God is true, our word toward you was not yea and nay. For the Son of God, Jesus Christ, who was preached among you by us, even by me and Silvanus and Timotheus, was not yea and nay, but **in Him was yea. For all the promises of God in Him are yea, and in Him Amen, unto the glory of God by us.**"*

Matthew 8:16, 17 (KJV) says, *'When the even was come, they brought unto him many that were possessed with devils: and he cast out the spirits with his word, and healed all that were ill: That it might be fulfilled which was spoken by Esaias the prophet, saying, "HIMSELF TOOK OUR INFIRMITIES, AND BARE OUR SICKNESSES."*

Even when we go back to Isaiah 53:4-5 to which this Scripture is referring, it says: *Surely our griefs He Himself bore, And our sorrows He carried; yet we ourselves esteemed Him stricken, smitten of God, and afflicted. But He was pierced through for our transgressions, He was crushed for our iniquities; the chastening for our well-being fell on Him, and by His scourging we are healed."*

The words, "griefs" and "sorrows" in the Hebrew are "*makob*[14]" and "*choli*[15]" which actually means physical <u>pain</u> and <u>sickness</u>.

---

[14] http://biblehub.com/hebrew/4341.htm
[15] http://biblehub.com/hebrew/2483.htm

Also, in I Peter 2:24 (KJV) *"Who His own self bare our sins in His own body on the tree, that we, being dead to sins,* **should live** *unto righteousness:* **by whose stripes ye were healed.**"

By the stripes that Jesus bore on His back on the Cross, we **were healed** of every sickness, disease, infirmity, and affliction. **It all went on Him!** If we want Jesus to receive the full honor and glory for His suffering on our behalf, then we need to appropriate—by faith—<u>everything</u> that He suffered on the Cross to obtain for us! Furthermore, we must not only believe for ourselves but also for others.

In Mark 16:15-18 (KJV), it says, *"......Go ye into all the world, and preach the Gospel to every creature. He that believeth and is baptized shall be saved; but he that believeth not shall be damned. And these signs shall follow them that believe; in My name shall they cast out devils; they shall speak with new tongues; they shall take up serpents; and if they drink any deadly thing, it shall not hurt them; they shall lay hands on the sick, and they shall recover."*

Paul prayed over handkerchiefs and aprons and sent them out to the people according to Acts 19:11, 12 (KJV). *"And God wrought special miracles by the hands of Paul so that from his body were brought unto the sick handkerchiefs or aprons, and the* **diseases** *departed from them, and the evil spirits went out of them."*

Throughout the week prior to my scheduled heart catheterization, I also listened to teaching tapes on healing by Nasir Sidikki.[16] It's a good practice to listen to teaching from the Word of God whenever possible, even when we aren't in a crisis. There are always nuggets of truth that we can glean from. God has put each of us, as members of the body of Christ, to be of assistance one to another and revelation given to each for the edification of those who are connected one with another. To you, my own dear readers, I am hopeful that many of you have been able to glean nuggets of Truth from the things that I am feeling led to share throughout the pages of this book. Nuggets of Truth that can grow your faith and help to direct your path.

During the night prior to my appointment, the Holy Spirit was reminding me that we are not sicknesses trying to get healed; **we are the healed, throwing lying symptoms back at the devil!** Sandra Kennedy[17] says, "If God thinks I'm healed, and I think I'm sick; then somebody's confused, and it isn't God!"

Then more toward morning, I heard God say to me, **"I'm giving you a Christmas miracle!"** Still, I kept the appointment for the heart catheterization. During the procedure, I allowed myself to think only one thing, "The same resurrection power that raised Jesus from the dead is operating in me! The same DNA that is in Jesus' blood is traveling through my arteries and veins, and it is the power that is

---

[16] Nasir Sidikki: After his own miraculous healing He teach God's Word and Wisdom all over the world.

[17] Sandra Kennedy: Accepting a mandate by God to "grow up the Body of Christ and teach them victory" in spirit, soul, and body.

in Jesus' blood that is breaking through every narrow place, every clogged place, making me every bit whole!

Immediately after the procedure one of the nurses went in to where my daughters were waiting for me and gave them the report. **"There is no blockage, no narrowing, and no coronary artery disease!"** I never saw a doctor after that. **Glory to God the Father, His Son our Lord Jesus Christ, and the Holy Spirit!**

A few days later, I went onto *The Elijah List* website and read an article by Steve Shultz[18] where he was saying, **"Christmas is swirling all around us right now!"** Steve had prophesied this after arriving home to the aroma of Christmas spices like cinnamon and nutmeg from cookies his wife Derene had been baking. I immediately understood that as confirmation to what I heard God speaking to me early in the morning on the appointed day of my own "Christmas miracle" on April 2nd! With God all things are possible! With God we can have Christmas any day of the year!

It is common after we experience the manifestation of healing in our bodies for the enemy to come back later and try to put those same symptoms back on us. When we receive confirmations such as this one by Steve Shultz, it strengthens us in our commitment and capability to stand. Thank God for the gifts of the Spirit that operate within each member of the body of Christ! Every gift of the Holy Spirit carries PURPOSE!

> The Apostle Paul admonishes us to stand against the enemy in Ephesians 6:11-20: *"Put on the full armor of God, so that you will be able to stand firm*

---

[18] Steve Shultz: founder and publisher of ***The Elijah List*** the non-denominational Christian prophetic website www.elijahlist.com

against the schemes of the devil. For our struggle is not against flesh and blood, but against the rulers, against the powers, against the world forces of this darkness, against the spiritual forces of wickedness in the heavenly places. Therefore, take up the full armor of God, so that you will be able to resist in the evil day, and having done everything, to stand firm. Stand firm therefore, HAVING GIRDED YOUR LOINS WITH TRUTH, AND HAVING PUT ON THE BREASTPLATE OF RIGHTEOUSNESS, and having shod YOUR FEET WITH THE PREPARATION OF THE GOSPEL OF PEACE; in addition to all, taking up the shield of faith with which you will be able to extinguish all the flaming arrows of the evil one. And take THE HELMET OF SALVATION, and the sword of the Spirit, which is the word of God.

With all prayer and petition pray at all times in the Spirit, and with this in view, be on the alert with all perseverance and petition for all the saints, and pray on my behalf, that utterance may be given to me in the opening of my mouth, to make known with boldness the mystery of the Gospel, for which I am an ambassador in chains; that in proclaiming it I may speak boldly, as I ought to speak."

When the fall season came around that year, I went back to the original doctor I had seen because I wanted him to give me a prescription for something to use on a rash that had developed around my ankle, leg, and knee. While I was in his office, I asked him to confirm to me that what happened to me in April was a miracle from God. He checked my file. We can't expect our doctors to remember who we are or what took place when they saw us, especially when we get referred to other specialists. After reviewing my records, he confirmed, "Yes! That would have been a miracle!" Once he realized that I believe in healing, he said, "You shouldn't even be looking at that. You shouldn't even be calling that a rash." Well, he was right!

Then he went on to share with me how he had been diagnosed with cancer at the same time I was going through what I went through, and he and his wife went to a healing ministry in Texas for prayer covering, teaching on the Word of God, and personal faith-building. **There was no more cancer!** In fact, they had been there four times throughout the year; and every time they went, they were healed of something else! I thought he was writing a prescription for prednisone to give to me after that, but instead he was jotting down the website address of the ministry he and his wife had been attending, *The Living Savior Ministries*, Thurman Scrivner[19], Argyle, TX.

We also had a brief discussion about how healing <u>comes from the inside out</u>. Sin and sickness are linked together and we need to deal with issues of the heart like *unforgiveness, bitterness, resentment, etc.* which can be hindrances to receiving the full manifestation of our healing.

> James 5:14-16 says, *"Is anyone among you sick? Then he must call for the elders of the church and they are to pray over him, anointing him with oil in*

---

[19] Thurman Scrivner: Pastor of *The Living Savior Ministries*, Argyle, TX.

the name of the Lord; and the prayer offered in faith will restore the one who is sick, and the Lord will raise him up, and if he has committed sins, they will be forgiven him. Therefore, confess your sins to one another, and pray for one another so that you may be healed. The effective prayer of a righteous man can accomplish much."

One of the things that we need to do <u>often</u> is to **take inventory** of what we have stored up in our hearts. If there is anything like unforgiveness, resentment, hatred, or a root of bitterness toward anyone we need to <u>let it go</u>. These are things we need to nip in the bud because if we allow any of these attributes to take root and grow, we put ourselves on dangerous ground and open ourselves up to sickness and disease.

Fear is another deadly enemy. We can be operating in fear without being aware that it is fear we are entertaining. The enemy camouflages the thoughts he sends to us in so many various forms that we can fall into agreement with his lies, having no realization of what they are actually rooted in. **As we pray in the spirit, the Holy Spirit can put a light on these strongholds and help us to pluck up, pull up, and cast them down.**

<u>Moving past the hindrance of fear</u>

At the age of 65 my brother-in-law Tom underwent surgery related to an aneurism and failed to come out of the anesthetic. Instead, he remained in a semi-conscious state in the ICU for the period of a full month. My sister reported to me on a daily basis as she and her husband Tom's brother were visiting him in the hospital. They were unable to converse with him. Because he was fighting the nurses and others on staff any time they tried to administer treatment to him, they had him strapped to the bed.

After a month, my sister Janice was told he was being moved to a different facility. She needed to sign release papers the next day and, at the same time, she was informed by his therapist that he had an *infection in the brain*—which was the reason he had remained in this semi-conscious state for so many days. No one had told her of the infection up until then.

I had thought about going to the hospital to pray for Tom but talked myself out of it because I didn't want to get that close to someone who was acting violently. When I heard he was being moved to some nursing home type facility, I decided I would go to the ICU and lay hands on him and pray like the Bible tells us to do. After all, he was strapped down so how could he hurt me?

I went in the afternoon of the day prior to his scheduled transfer date. He was in a connecting room off to the side of the main ICU and no one saw me go in. **I took authority over every demon spirit I could think of and commanded the spirits to go out of him in the NAME of JESUS!** Yet Tom seemed oblivious to the fact that I was there.

Early the next morning, Janice—along with Tom's brother—went to the hospital. Both were of the same mind, that Tom wasn't going to be any different than he was the day before and the day before that. Instead, they found Tom sitting up on the edge of the bed talking with four doctors who were **releasing him TO GO HOME!** They were both in disbelief! Janice headed back home to get street clothes for Tom and called me to come pick him up in my SUV while his brother couldn't wait to get his wife on his cell phone to tell her what had happened!

When I got there, a nurse was helping Tom pack his things. She pulled the former release form—releasing him to the nursing facility—out of his file and said, "Well, he's not going to need this!" Then she voiced a mathematical question aloud which seemed rather complicated to me. Tom began punching numbers on his watch calculator, and the nurse laid everything down. She leaned back from the erect position she had been sitting in and said, **"I still can't believe all he is able to do!"**

Upon returning home, Tom went back to playing his guitar. This was something he'd been away from for many years. Not only that, but for the first time in his life, he started playing **praise and worship songs and singing along with worship leaders/teams on television!**

Purposing to stay in forgiveness

My son, Jason, shared an experience with me not long ago where he and his wife were riding their bicycles along a country road. An obviously irritated driver roared the engine of his pickup truck as he sped up heading toward Jason at an angle. It frightened Bridget because she was riding behind a short distance and thought the pickup was going to hit Jason. Thank the Lord that did not happen. However, what did happen angered both of them!

On the somewhat foggy morning after, Jason was riding alone. He had gotten such a good look at the pickup truck, he knew he would recognize it if he saw it in a driveway along the route. He was on watch for it; and he was still angry. He was angry enough to do something about it if, per chance, he spotted it anywhere.

But then, he rode past an older gentleman who was putting his garbage cans out at the foot of his driveway. As Jason flew by him on his bicycle, the man said, **"Be careful, Son!"** Goose bumps went over Jason as the words from this obviously very kind man penetrated into the built-up anger that had been propelling him only seconds before. Just the thought that there are people out here who are good and kind, in spite of the few who are not so yielding, made it possible for Jason to immediately drop the anger he had been harboring from the previous day's experience. He turned back to the man in the driveway and said, **"God bless you, Sir!"**

When Bridget brought it up later that day, still thinking someone needed to knock that guy up the side of the head with a baseball bat, Jason said, "I've already forgiven him." Then Bridget forgave him as well! The next time I talked with Jason's dad, I told him that the older gentleman might have been placed there by an angel. His quick response: **"Maybe _he_ was an angel!"**

Personal Notes: In order for the body of Christ to stay Kingdom-minded, we need to have a steady diet of fresh daily Word to sustain us in difficult places. Every miracle recorded in God's Word is for us to glean from and to experience our own Faith being strengthened thereby. Faith comes by hearing, and hearing by the Word of God! It is necessary to speak the Word of God and meditate on the Scriptures in order for the Holy Spirit to have something to work with when we are facing situations of a complex nature. We can go back in time and pick up miracles from our past, reminding the Lord of what He did for us before, as we come before Him in faith believing for Him to show Himself alive in us all over again.

Chapter Six

Wisdom In Relationships

The LORD designed human beings with a need for companionship. We were not intended to exist in isolation. Time and time again He has shown us that *relationships*—especially our relationship with Him—are vitally important. They create a support system that is good for our physical and spiritual health and well-being, and science has proven that good relationships actually increase our longevity. However, what we face in today's world of technology, religious, philosophical and social divisiveness is an everyday challenge.

We are all aware that social networking is changing how people relate one to another. Those who once shared a close relationship have expressed a noticeable disconnect. Through social networking, the *number* of people we keep in touch with has expanded while relationships among those who were once close have suffered. I've heard some comments from people that, "We don't **visit** anymore." "When we were visiting in person, it was easier to understand where our discussion was going." "Text messages can be so easily misunderstood when the tone of what is being relayed is not that obvious."

Perhaps some of you who are reading this may be among those who have expressed a sense of similar isolation over a period of time. Yet, we must admit that social networking has been playing a huge role in the furtherance of the Gospel into regions around the globe where many souls have been reached that may not have been otherwise. We, who make up the body of Christ, have likewise received encouragement, training, and insight through the articles that have now been *posted* at our fingertips on a daily basis. Everyone who has access to a computer can now receive daily updates from those who function within the prophet/seer anointing, fulfilling a crucial role as God's mouthpiece to the modern-day Church. There is no way to measure the value this has added to the growth of the Church or the furtherance of the Gospel into some of the darkest regions where perhaps no minister or preacher of the Word of God has traveled to personally.

Either way we look at it, whether we are pointing out pros or cons, social networking is here to stay. How many of us are especially grateful for the rekindled connections to family and friends that has opened a window into the lives and activities of our parents, mates, children and grandchildren. Indeed, many of us are experiencing improved <u>family</u> relationships <u>because</u> we can communicate with each other by text, email, <u>and</u> cellphone.

<u>Common interests</u> can serve as tools that bring people together. As much as we might feel we have become a part in the joint activities, interests, endeavors, and like-goals of various groups, there may be <u>seasons</u> when we need to sit back and examine the individual role

that we ourselves are playing within that circle of people. We may be *going with the flow*, so to speak, with the assumption that God is pleased—or at least okay—with the fact that we are involved in the group activities. Some might believe that God is not interested in having a voice in the "trivial" things that take up our day. However, what if God <u>does care</u> and is willing to show us a bigger picture of where He is taking us within our club/group relationships. If our steps are truly ordered of the Lord—according to His Word—then <u>He does care</u>, doesn't He?

I believe many are "sitting it out" so to speak in hopes that something big from God will happen to them that will bring sudden change into their lives, fixing everything. I did that for years. It didn't work! We can receive a revelation showing us the big picture God has for us, but we can't ignore the fact that He might be requiring <u>us</u> to <u>go through a process</u> to get there. This process could be over a long period of time that involves people connections that are group related.

If an unpleasant incident occurs, as it easily can from time to time, we work through it and maintain our place in the group. These might feel like little bumps in the road, and who among us does not experience a few unpleasant encounters from time to time. It's those times, when we experience the *tearing away at the rubber on the tire*, that we find ourselves sitting back to evaluate what we are really doing there. What are we to gain from the relationship? Where is this relationship really going? Many people stay in these group relationships because they feel that they are needed—people are depending on them—or just that others are happy to have them be a part of their gatherings.

We have life-long friendships that go back to our growing up years in school, or those who we might have worked with right out of school, and these are friendships that we hold very dear. They are also very hard to give up when they are no longer with us due to unpredicted illnesses, etc. I had to say farewell to two such special people in my life over the last several months leaving a huge vacuum that can't be replenished by any other.

I recently spoke with one of my life-long friends, and the subject came up in our conversation about how we are to respond to friends or even relatives who—by their own actions—make it clear that they have placed us on the back burner of their lives. They say they are going to call us and never do. They are happy that we can now email, but they never do. If we email them, they don't respond. If they do respond, it's a month later, and what we wrote is no longer relevant. Surprisingly, my friend and I had to admit that, perhaps, we've even been this kind of friend to others.

All of these thoughts about relationship groups brought my thinking back to JESUS and His own disciples. Many of them were friends before they became disciples. Some were even brothers of the same families prior to JESUS' call on their lives to be followers of Him. Yet when they met Him, they <u>walked away</u> from the majority of their close relationships. JESUS became the center of their lives. IN this new relationship, how much were they able to comprehend that this JESUS—Who was making such a **profound impact** on <u>their</u> lives—would be IMPACTING THE ENTIRE WORLD for ETERNITY?

Next, I wondered, HOW committed are <u>we</u> in our *relationship with JESUS?* Are we comfortable enough in that relationship with Him to bring JESUS into our relationships one with another? If we have a disagreement do we ask ourselves, "What would JESUS do?" Would there be a SHIFTING taking place in relationships we have become involved in over the years IF we were to begin to **decree** over our days that **we have a heart and a listening ear to be led by the Holy Spirit?** Are we willing to walk away from certain relationships if they involve friends of ours who are not willing to go where we desire to go in our relationship with Jesus?

> The Apostle Peter says in his letter, I Peter 4:3-6, *"For the time already past is sufficient for you to have carried out the desire of the Gentiles, having pursued a course of sensuality, lusts, drunkenness, carousing, drinking parties and abominable idolatries. In all this,* ***they are surprised that you do not run with them into the same excesses of dissipation, and they malign you;*** *but they will give account to Him who is ready to judge the living and the dead. For the Gospel has for this purpose been preached even to those who are dead, that though they are judged in the flesh as men, they may live in the spirit according to the will of God."*

There is also much to be said about <u>personal relationships</u> in the **Book of Proverbs.**

~ Proverbs 16:24: *"Pleasant words are a honeycomb, sweet to the soul and healing to the bones."*

- Proverbs 16:28: *"A perverse man spreads strife, And a slanderer separates intimate friends."*
- Proverbs 17:9: *"He who conceals a transgression seeks love, but he who repeats a matter separates intimate friends."*
- Proverbs 18:19: *"A brother offended is harder to be won than a strong City, And contentions are like the bars of a citadel."*

Proverbs about Loyal Friendships:

- Proverbs 18:24: *"A man of too many friends comes to ruin, but there is a friend who sticks closer than a brother."*
- Proverbs 27:6: *"Faithful are the wounds of a friend, but deceitful are the kisses of an enemy."*
- Proverbs 27:9: *"Oil and perfume make the heart glad, so a man's counsel is sweet to his friends."*
- Proverbs 27:10: *"Do not forsake your own friend or your father's friend, and do not go to your brother's house in the day of your calamity; better is a neighbor who is near than a brother far away."*
- Proverbs 27:14: *"He who blesses his friend with a loud voice early in the morning, It will be reckoned a curse to him."*
- Proverbs 27:17: *"Iron sharpens iron, so one man sharpens another."*
- Proverbs 26:18, 19: *"Like a madman who throws firebrands, arrows and death, So is the man who deceives his neighbor, and says, 'Was I not Joking'."*
- Proverbs 25:8-10: *"Do not go out hastily to argue your case; otherwise, what will you do in the end when your neighbor humiliates you?"*

- Proverbs 25:17: *"Let your foot rarely be in your neighbor's house, or he will become weary of you and hate you."*
- Proverbs 25:19: *"Like a bad tooth and an unsteady foot is confidence in an unfaithful man in time of trouble."*
- Proverbs 19:22: *"What is desirable in a man is kindness, and it is better to be a poor man than a liar."*
- Proverbs 20:6: *"Many a man proclaims his own loyalty, but who can find a trustworthy man?"*
- Proverbs 14:22: *"Will they not go astray who devise evil? But kindness and truth will be to those who devise good."*
- Proverbs 13:20: *"He who walks with wise men will be wise, but the companion of fools will suffer harm."*

So, would it not be <u>best</u> to **bring GOD into our personal relationships** and pray for Him to give us the Spirit of Wisdom and Understanding, the Spirit of Counsel and Might, and the Spirit of Knowledge of the LORD JESUS CHRIST as well as the Fear (*reverence*) of the LORD! In I Peter 4:17-19, we are reminded that we ourselves have scarcely been saved, and judgement begins with the household of God. Then, if it begins with us first, what will be the outcome for those who do not obey the Gospel of Jesus Christ?

In the Book of Ezekiel, Chapter 33: 8-9, God warns those whom He has set as ***watchmen*** over the house of Israel that they are to warn the wicked to turn from their wicked ways. If they refused to hear the messenger, then their blood will be on their own hands. However, if the watchmen fail to <u>give</u> warning, and that person dies in his iniquity, that man's blood will be required from his hand. In other words, by warning the wicked, we save our own souls from destruction.

> In Ezekiel 33:11, God says: *"Say to them, 'As I live!' declares the Lord GOD, 'I take no pleasure in the death of the wicked, but rather that the wicked turn from his way and live..........'"*

Today, we need to be warning the <u>LOST</u> that JESUS' return to earth is **imminent**, lest we be held accountable to GOD for missed opportunities to present the Gospel of *grace* to them.

> Romans 5:8, 9: *"But God demonstrates His own love toward us, in that while we were yet sinners, Christ died for us. Much more then, having now been justified by His blood, we shall be saved from the wrath of God through Him."*

That is CHRIST JESUS!

If we are going to operate in **Wisdom** from GOD, we need to keep our **spiritual antennas** up. I was reminded of this just recently at a time when I had failed to keep a listening ear attuned to the HOLY SPIRIT's *still small voice*. This resulted in my having to go to a close friend and apologize for burdening her further when she was already feeling the burden of a bad report from the doctor relating to her husband's health.

When we have many years of teaching under our belts regarding God's principles of healing, I don't believe I am alone in this temptation to *pounce on every wrong confession* that comes out of the mouth of other believers. When they happen NOT to be adhering constantly to speaking the Word of God **ONLY**, could it be that we are being too legalistic to *insist that they do* regardless of any stressful news they might have been handed?

> In I Peter 4:8, 9, we are told, *"Above all, keep fervent in your **LOVE** for one another...."*

Secondly, not every member in the body of Christ is "eating" the *meat* of the Word, so to speak. Hebrews 5:13,14 addresses the subject that some are still on *milk* as compared to infants who are receiving huge amounts of nutrition, but are unable to understand many things.

> *"For everyone who partakes only of milk is not accustomed to the word of righteousness, for he is an infant. But solid food is for the mature, who because of practice have their senses trained to discern good and evil."*

I John 4:7, 11, 12, 16 and 20 (consecutively) tells us, *"Beloved, let us love one another, for love is from God; and everyone who loves is born of God and knows God." "Beloved, if God so loved us, we also ought to love one another." "No one has seen God at any time; if we love one another, God abides in us, and His love is perfected in us." "We have come to know and have believed the love which God has for us. God is love, and the one who abides in love abides in God, and God abides in him." "If someone says,*

> *'I love God' and hates his brother, he is a liar; for the one who does not love his brother whom he has seen, cannot love God whom he has not seen."*

Yet, this doesn't disregard the fact that the Church is hurting for "<u>militant minds</u>" **who will *stand against the wiles of the devil*.** It behooves us to pursue as much teaching on spiritual warfare **as** we can, **while** we can, because the devil isn't standing back waiting.

When circumstances become overwhelming, it is God's will that we continue to stay in forgiveness. Quite often we could find ourselves facing situations where it is impossible to forgive in our natural strength. For example, if we view a situation as being unjust, we are saying in a sense that God is an unjust God. Yet, His Word says that God is a <u>just and fair</u> God so we need to **come into agreement with what His Word says in order for Him to intervene in our behalf**. This is spiritual warfare as we fight the good fight of faith. To go from viewing a situation in the natural to viewing it from the standpoint of God's Word may be viewed by God as—you and I—taking **a giant leap of Faith!**

> *"Finally, be strong in the Lord and in the strength of his might. Put on the full armor of God, so that you will be able to stand firm against the schemes of the devil. For our struggle is not against flesh and blood, but against the rulers, against the powers, against the world forces of this darkness, against the spiritual forces of wickedness in the heavenly places. Therefore, take up the full armor of God, so that you*

will be able to resist in the evil day, and having done everything, to stand firm." (Ephesians 6:10-13)

So, how can we learn more about GOD's ways regarding personal friendships? How can we practice His Wisdom, Love and Understanding within friendships that challenge us from time to time? Even when all seems to be going smoothly, is that friend-relationship where GOD wants it to be? Is it possible for us to be linked in relationships that are keeping us from growing at a pace we might be more apt to grow in if we were planted elsewhere?

In the School of the HOLY SPIRIT, there are different classrooms and many levels of learning. In Colossians 1, beginning with verse 9, the Apostle Paul wrote,

"For this reason also, since the day we heard of it, we have not ceased to pray for you and to ask that you may be filled with knowledge of His will in all spiritual wisdom and understanding, so that you will walk in a manner worthy of the Lord, to please Him in all respects, **bearing fruit in every good work and increasing in the knowledge of God;** *strengthened with all power, according to His glorious might, for* **the attaining of all steadfastness and patience;** *joyously giving thanks to the Father, who has qualified us to share in the inheritance of the saints in Light."*

In Romans 1:13, Paul expressed in writing how he had often planned to go to them but had been prevented from doing so. His purpose was in hopes of both he and they being equally encouraged by one another's faith. Paul expressly mentioned that by imparting some spiritual gift to them, he might obtain some **fruit** among them. In Luke 6:44, we read Jesus' words...

> *"For each tree is known by its own fruit. For men do not gather figs from thorns, nor do they pick grapes from a briar bush. The good man out of the good treasure of his heart brings forth what is good; and the evil man out of the evil treasure brings forth what is evil; for his mouth speaks from that which fills his heart."*

The fruit of the SPIRIT is love, joy, peace, patience, kindness, goodness, faithfulness, gentleness, and self-control. JESUS gave us this parable in Luke 13:6-9...

> *"A man had a fig tree which had been planted in his vineyard; and he came looking for fruit on it and did not find any, and he said to the vineyard-keeper, 'Behold, for three years I have come looking for fruit on this fig tree without finding any. Cut it down! Why does it even use up the ground?' And he answered and said to him, 'Let it alone, sir, for this year too, until I dig around it and put in fertilizer; and if it bears fruit next year, fine; but if not, cut it down.'"*

As we carry this metaphor into personal relationships, how are we to know when—in the dry, rough seasons of our relationships—whether or not this might be a <u>*part of the process necessary*</u> to bring us into the *fruit bearing season*? JESUS also said in John 15 that <u>He</u>

is the <u>True Vine</u> and <u>His Father is the Vinedresser</u>. Every branch in Him that does not bear fruit He takes away, and every plant that does bear fruit, He **prunes it so that it will bear more fruit**. This implies that we might be going through spiritual inspection at times, **but how are we to know** if we are being watered, pruned, fertilized, or cut down? Hopefully not cut down, but the pruning process indicates we are going to be going through a measure of *discomfort* at least.

Several years ago, I had a night vision where I was observing two men who were watering plants in a greenhouse. Most of the plants appeared to be similar in height, around four or five feet tall. However, they came to one plant that was still in the pot yet had grown almost to the ceiling! Their first thought seemed to be to skip over that plant because it was already so much taller than any of the other plants in the greenhouse. But then, on second thought, because they were there anyway they decided to give it some water after all. So why did **I** have that vision? The only conclusion I came to was that this must be me **still here in this greenhouse** and still no fruit evident as far up as I could see! I've been working on being a fruit-bearing servant of God ever since.

One group I was involved with resulted in several relationships that continued after I was no longer a part of the group. Because of one incident, I had pulled out of this group thinking at the time that I was making this decision of my own volition. However; within a day or so of my leaving, I had a dream where I was seated with this group in the living room of one of the homes where we had been meeting. JESUS walked in and came right over to where I was seated, took me by the hand, and marched me right out without saying a word! It was only then that I came to realize that JESUS had taken me out of there!

Not long after that experience I heard one of my favorite television preachers preaching about this same thing. He was sharing how <u>GOD puts us with different people for and during specific seasons in our lives</u>. Some of his contacts with friends and groups had been for short seasons, some over longer seasons, and at one particular time the LORD came in and literally **yanked** him right out of the group he was in! At this, I thought, "Yep. Been there, done that!"

How apt are we to fall short at times of other's expectations of us? Perhaps because we failed to attend a social event? Does this mean we have to "face the music" afterward if the reason we gave happened to be one that wasn't suitable to our friend who would have liked to have had more of an influence over our decision to pass on the invitation? Does this have to mean that we are now in a position of having to be chastised in some fashion—given the silent treatment over a period of time—until this friend feels they have been proportionately appeased? It was several months into a similar fallout of repercussion when I heard in my spirit, "You are **being strengthened to shake the dust.**"

Right after hearing this in my spirit, Rodney Howard-Brown[20] was sharing on television how he had his driver pull the car off the side of the road as they were leaving a city so that he could get out and <u>*shake the dust off his shoes*</u> from that city. He actually got out of the car and clapped the soles of his shoes together in demonstration of knocking the dust off them. Then he said, "If I'd had a vacuum, I would have vacuumed the floorboard of the car just to make sure no

---

[20] Rodney Howard-Brown: founder of ***Revival Ministries International.***

dust was left there that might have fallen from my shoes." It could be that *dust* is symbolic of the mental tossing we have a natural tendency to put ourselves through—because of actions or lack of actions on the part of others when sometimes we need to just move on.

I'm not suggesting that either of the above examples are to be carried out **randomly** because we are not to judge people or situations outwardly in our own human logic. In John 7:24, Jesus said, *"Do not judge according to appearance, but judge with righteous judgment."*

Within the context of the Church, Paul the Apostle states very clearly the importance each member plays in the Body of CHRIST. In I Corinthians 12:14-26, we can read...

> *"For the body is not one member, but many. If the foot says, 'Because I am not a hand, I am not a part of the body,' it is not for this reason any the less a part of the body. And if the ear says, 'Because I am not an eye, I am not a part of the body,' it is not for this reason any the less a part of the body. If the whole body were an eye, where would the hearing be? If the whole were hearing, where would the sense of smell be? But now God has placed the members, each one of them, in the body, just as He desired. If they were all one member, where would the body be? But now there are many members, but one body. And the eye cannot say to the hand, 'I have no need of you'; or again the head to the feet, 'I have no need of you.' On the contrary, it is much truer that the members of the body which seem to be weaker are necessary; and those members of the body which we deem less*

honorable, on these we bestow more abundant honor, and our less presentable members become much more presentable, whereas our more presentable members have no need of it. But God has so composed the body, giving more abundant honor to that member which lacked, so that there may be no division in the body, but that the members may have the same care for one another. And if one member suffers, all the members suffer with it; if one member is honored, all the members rejoice with it."

If we fail to remain prayerful or fail to view where we are in relationships one with another with the help of the HOLY SPIRIT, we may be cutting off a hand or an ear or a tip of a finger in GOD's eyes. The Word of GOD tells us that we are to <u>esteem others</u> more highly than ourselves. (See Philippians 2:3) Yet His Word also prepares us to step away from relationships when the time is right. *"For everything there is a season, and a time for every matter under heaven...."* (Ecclesiastes 3:1).

In Acts 14:39,40 we see where Paul and Barnabas went their separate ways after a sharp dispute—Paul went with Silas, and Barnabas took Mark with him—yet they may have been brought back together in another season.

In I Corinthians 13:12 the Word tells us that *now we see in a mirror dimly, but then face to face what we now know in part shall be fully known just as we have been fully known.* In our Faith walk, we are given bits and pieces as we continue moving forward into what GOD has prepared for us. None of us can be **fully aware** of everything that is transpiring in our own walk with the LORD, let alone try to understand what GOD is doing in the lives of others except by the gifts of the HOLY SPIRIT in operation. This might occur through *a word of knowledge* or *the gift of prophecy* such as when the prophet Agabus took Paul's belt and bound his own feet and hands. Then he said, "This is what the HOLY SPIRIT says: 'In this way the Jews at Jerusalem will bind the man who owns this belt and deliver him into the hands of the Gentiles.'" (See Acts 21:10-11)

The Apostle Peter had a very special relationship with Jesus. One recorded conversation between them is very eye-opening because it exposes a bit of jealousy Peter held toward John (John 21:15-22). When Peter notices John in the group, Peter asks Jesus, *"What shall this man do?"* Jesus response was, *"What is that to you? You follow me."* You see, sometimes we are let in on things, and sometimes we aren't. We aren't meant to know everything that is being wrought by the SPIRIT OF GOD in the lives of others, only what GOD opens our eyes and understanding to see, and know, for His own purposes. Even when Jesus joined up with Cleopas and another walking with him right after His resurrection (Luke 24:13-27), the Bible says their eyes were *prevented* from recognizing who Jesus was for that moment in time. In Matthew 17:12, Jesus told His disciples that Elijah had already come—meaning John the Baptist—**but the scribes did not recognize him and did to him whatever they wished.**

We can look at what all Joseph—the son of Israel's patriarch, Jacob—went through prior to the **GOD appointed moment** when Joseph announced to his brothers that it was GOD Himself who had sent him before them to preserve their lives by a great deliverance! He assured them that it was **not them** who sent him there to Pharaoh's house, but GOD! Even though in the natural, they had sold him off to slavery; he told them not to grieve or be angry with themselves because it was all a part of GOD's plan. (See Genesis 45)

How many times might Joseph have questioned some of the things he had to endure throughout all those years—in between the dreams GOD had given him at such a young age—and <u>his GOD appointed destiny</u> coming to fruition? When Joseph interpreted the dream for Pharaoh's chief butler in prison, Joseph wanted him to *make mention* of him to Pharaoh when all was well with him. It was still another two long years before the butler remembered to tell Pharaoh about Joseph's ability to interpret dreams.

How many of us might start out trying to believe GOD to get us out of a jam and throw in the towel in the <u>first</u> year? We don't want to hear that GOD might have such an endurance test for us to have to go through. Forget any suggestion that it might continue for decades! Was there anyone in that prison with Joseph who might have thought for a moment that **GOD** had a call on Joseph's life? Chances were likely that Joseph himself may have lost sight of **GOD's call** which he felt so certain of when the dreams as a young lad were still fresh in his mind. He probably wondered a thousand times over if he might have spared himself years of agony had he kept quiet to his family about those dreams in the first place.

The Scriptures refer to another young lad who followed after JESUS in the Garden of Gethsemane after all His <u>disciples</u> **had left Him and fled!** The lad was wearing nothing but a linen sheet over his naked body when the young men in the crowd who came to capture JESUS laid hold on him. He left the linen cloth and fled from them naked. That's all the Bible has to say about this young man who showed such boldness to still hang around after JESUS' own followers had taken off in fear for their lives. (See Mark 14:51-52)

I had a dream many years ago about this same young lad. The dream began with me standing at an upstairs window of a building that resembled those common to that region. It was a square open window, no glass, no screen. Off in the distance, I could see Golgotha's Hill with three crosses. Then the scene changed, and I found myself standing at the foot of the Cross that JESUS was on. There was a crowd of men and soldiers yelling, mocking, and throwing stones at Him! Then this young lad—the same young boy who is spoken of in the Gospel of Mark—went charging into this wild crowd shouting for them to stop! "STOP IT, STOP IT, STOP IT!" JESUS, witnessing what was happening, began to say something in **a language I couldn't understand**. Even though I had no comprehension of what JESUS said, I knew it was meant for this young boy who was challenging the actions of the crowd that had gathered. I knew what JESUS was saying was something good about him.

Very close to me was one of JESUS' disciples who was also hearing the words of JESUS. He **did understand the language** and thought that JESUS meant those words for him! Yet I knew JESUS' words were meant for this faithful young lad who had stayed by Him in the garden even after His disciples had forsaken Him in fear. I can't help but think this might have really happened just like I saw it in the dream.

When I awoke, the profound impact of that close and faithful relationship between this young man and JESUS remained with me. We are all invited to know the same.

One of the longest relationships I've had over the years is with a person who has been more like the brother I never had. Likewise, I might be like the sister he never had. It wasn't long into this relationship that I began to realize the HOLY SPIRIT was involved in bringing us together for the purpose of helping us both to <u>grow</u> in our Faith in GOD!

One of the first things I recall happening that caused me to come to this realization was when I woke up one morning hearing these words being spoken in my spirit: "There's a dog Steve likes going into the pound today." I had never been to the pound; but as the day progressed into afternoon, I decided to go there to see if I could pick out a dog Steve might like — one that just came in that day. Faith is a *process* in that we are only shown more as we move out in what we have already been given.

While strolling around in the pound, I came upon a big cage with a small dog standing all alone. He was muddy, wet, and looking all forlorn. I went to the desk and asked them if this little dog happened to have been brought in that day? They checked the card in the file and said, "Yes. He was brought in just after 2 p.m. today. He's a Shih-tzu."

Not willing to make any quick decisions on something I hadn't put any previous thought to, I went home without him. I decided to return the next morning and prayed, "LORD if You're in this, I would appreciate **some kind of sign** when I get there."

When I arrived that day, I drove up to a scene of people and pets standing outside the door waiting for the pound to open. With everyone scurrying in ahead of me, I soon found a young man willing to help me. I asked him if he could open the cage for me because I wanted to check out this little dog's disposition. As he proceeded to open the door to the cage, I couldn't help but notice the T-shirt he was wearing. It had a picture of a race car on it with the driver's name—"Steve Butler." This was Steve's first name and my last name! I immediately took it as the sign I had asked the LORD to give me if I was supposed to get this dog for Steve. So I did.

I took the dog home and gave him a bath because he was a mess. They told me he had been running around a neighborhood for several weeks with no place to get under shelter from the cold and rainy weather we had been having.

When I drove this little dog to Steve's house and he jumped out of the car, Steve's initial reaction wasn't what I expected. "If I would have picked out a dog for myself, I'd have found a man's dog!" he said. Even though he seemed at first not to be sold on this particular breed of dog, he quickly grew to love him <u>more</u> than any other dog he had ever had.

Three days later, we still had not come up with a name for the dog so I suggested to Steve he might want to pray for a name. We had tossed several lists of names back and forth; Steve didn't like my name suggestions, and I didn't go for any of his name suggestions. So he prayed rather reluctantly, "God, can you give us a name for this dog?"

The next morning, he remembered a vision he had as he was waking up. In the vision he was in an area where this little dog was wandering loose maybe twenty feet from where he was standing and talking with someone. He said, "Let's go, Tater." The dog came right to him, they walked off together, and Steve woke up. Steve said he knew I was going to like this name before he called to tell me about the vision. He was right. I thought the name was **perfect.** So **Tater** it was. (If this had been a longer drawn-out story in the night, I might be referring to it as a dream. However, in this case it was more like a *short movie clip* Steve saw as he was waking up which would be more like a vision than a dream.)

Steve and I were both encouraged with a deeper understanding that GOD cares about <u>everything</u> we are concerned about! Isn't it good to know that God is interested in the little things and He desires to meet us right where we are as opposed to the theology that He is too busy with all the big things He has to attend to? Yes, indeed, God will *meet us* and *care for us* no matter how muddied we are or how muddied our past.

The *seasons* of this friendship between Steve and I moved forward. One day, he was mowing my yard when the mower quit running. I had just finished reading a really good book written by a preacher of the post circuit-rider era. As Steve persisted in trying to figure out the problem with the mower, these words I'd just read came back to me, "If the solution to a given situation wasn't immediately available I would tell the people I didn't have the answer, but add that I would pray about it and have the answer by 7 o'clock the next morning." I immediately felt led to follow that example. So, while Steve was trying to figure out why the mower quit running, I went out and told him to leave it alone because I was going to pray about it and have the answer by 7 o'clock the next morning.

Leaving a job undone was a hard thing for Steve to do. Day turned into dark, and by then Steve had the owner's manual laid out on the garage floor. Two or three times, I went to the garage telling him to stop wasting his time trying to figure it out because I was going to pray about it and have the answer by 7 a.m. He finally gave up and went home.

I went to bed that evening and fell asleep before I got to pray about it. Nevertheless, as I was waking up the next morning, I was seeing a vision of a plug-in with prongs that had come unplugged under the dash where he hadn't been able to see it. I went to the garage, looked under the dash and there it was—hanging loose. I plugged it back in and started the mower! It was 7 a.m. when I stretched the long cord from my wall phone in the kitchen to the garage door so Steve could hear the sound of the engine running. He was so surprised because it happened just like I told him it would. GOD had blessed us both by demonstrating how we can rely on Him, walk in His peace and not allow our frustrations to waste precious time.

We might spend years in developing a "listening ear" to what the HOLY SPIRIT is saying to us. However, there's no assurance that when we relate what we hear in our spirits to other people that anyone is going to believe a word of it. Building confidence in *words* received from others—by the Holy Spirit—doesn't happen overnight. This reminds me of another incident that was shared in this same book mentioned above.

It was after GOD had spoken to this preacher telling him that the *season* had arrived for him to build the new home GOD had promised him. Someone in his congregation had given him a section of timber for the lumber he was going to need, but they had to cut down the trees and haul them to the saw mill. He had a lot of men helping him.

One day as they had finished loading a big stack of logs onto a truck, the preacher heard a **warning in his spirit that something was wrong**. He called out to the men to stand back away from the truck because something was wrong. They all stood back and waited. Nothing seemed amiss, and they told him they didn't see anything wrong. This preacher didn't see anything wrong either but knew he had heard correctly so ordered them to stay back. Then suddenly one of the chains snapped that was holding the logs on the back of the truck, and the logs went rolling off right where all the men had been standing! From that moment on, those men (and their families) were much more likely to put a greater degree of trust in what this preacher had to say to them!

God gives *gifts* of *insight* to preachers such as this one who have the mantles of pastor/shepherd. (See Romans 12:1-8) In these moments, people <u>see God's desire</u> to be a part of their daily lives as He seeks to bring them to repentance, redemption and everlasting Life.

One night I heard these words in <u>my</u> spirit: "911 Pray!" I didn't know what I was supposed to pray about but prayed anyway and found out the next day that at the same time I was being instructed to pray, one of my daughters was on her way home from McDonald's unaware that a strange man had gotten into her garage. I continue to thank God that there was no one-on-one confrontation because she didn't see him when she arrived home. The man, however, ended up in jail for a longer time than he had probably anticipated prior to his decision to break into her garage and cause $800 in damage to her vehicle when discovered by the police a short time later.

In I Thessalonians 5:17, we are told to *"pray without ceasing."* When I *heard* those words in my spirit, I knew someone, somewhere, was in need of the Lord's protection because of the familiar 911 emergency designation. The Holy Spirit works through what we *know*—what we have learned through experience and education. So it is vitally important that we keep learning and continue to seek His Wisdom in all things.

Some years later, I recall waking up one morning to the question, "How do little children fight the wizard of Oz?" My thinking was that they can't. Their parents must protect them from witchcraft including witchcraft that masquerades as entertainment.

When I saw my friend Steve later that day, I said, "I heard the strangest thing when I woke up this morning." When I told him what it was, **his mouth flew wide open!** He began telling me how he had not been able to get the song from that movie off his mind all day. He had seen the movie when he was a young child and now, many years later, was spending much of the day with those lyrics and music still playing over in his mind.

He went on to tell me that the only time he had ever been in the hospital in his life was the night after his family had seen that movie on television, and he had to spend the whole night there alone and away from his family. It was a very traumatic time for him to have to experience at such a young age.

Because of our conversation that day we wondered if perhaps this was the HOLY SPIRIT's way of putting light on a stronghold of the enemy that needed to be dealt with. That particular movie may not affect the majority of children/people in a negative way, however, something about it certainly held an adverse place in Steve's life. Curses—that which is meant to destroy or fight God's purposes in someone's life—have come onto families throughout generations from movies, books, board games, etc. that have found their way into people's homes. Today, more than ever, parents need to take responsibility for what their children are allowed to see or become involved in, especially when it comes to things like violent video games and the like. In Deuteronomy 18:9-12 we can read...

> *"When you enter the land which the LORD your God gives you, you shall not learn to imitate the detestable things of those nations. There shall not be found among you anyone who makes his son or his daughter pass through the fire, one who uses divination, one who practices witchcraft, or one who interprets omen, or a sorcerer, or one who casts a spell, or a medium, or a spiritist, or one who calls up the dead. For whoever does these things is detestable to the LORD; and because of these detestable things the LORD your God will drive them out before you."*

This occurrence sparked a keen awareness in both of us that there may also be <u>more</u> underlying curses that the Holy Spirit wanted to shed light on at that time. In Proverbs 20:2, Solomon establishes that behind every curse there is a cause. So what about generational curses? Steve and I learned that both our earthly fathers were involved in Freemasonry. We have since learned that Masonry is a false "religion" because it acknowledges false gods, namely two heathen deities—Baal and Osiris. Freemasonry <u>teaches that man is not sinful but merely imperfect, and therefore can redeem himself through good works</u>. Over many generations of warnings specifically regarding Freemasonry, it has been discovered "that the only belief requirement is <u>not</u> that one must believe in the True and Living

God, but rather, that one must believe in the existence of a "Supreme Being," which includes the "gods" of Islam, Hinduism, or any other world religion. The unbiblical and anti-Christian beliefs and practices of this organization are partially hidden beneath an outward appearance of a supposed compatibility with the Christian faith."

We needed to <u>renounce</u> former family involvement with Freemasonry—or any *system* that denies or waters-down God's Word—because any one of several generations' involvement could be the cause of a curse over our generation, let alone direct involvement by our immediate earthly fathers.

Now that I've given a little background of a few of the experiences Steve and I have shared along the way—demonstrating God's Faithfulness—I would like to share a bit more of what Steve has gone through in more recent years. These situations involve events that perhaps many reading this book will be able to relate to on a more personal level and Steve has given me permission to share them with you here.

After being turned down for several job positions and expressing to me his discouragement in trying to find work, I prayed and heard in my spirit, **"Steve is being moved into a great new job!"** From that time on, every time he told me what wasn't happening, I said to him, **"I don't care! All I <u>know</u> is that you are being moved into a great new job!"** This went on for weeks on end. Over and over, he complained about what wasn't happening. Over and over, I told him the same thing. **"I don't care! All I <u>know</u> is that you are being moved into a great new job!"**

Then one day he decided to fill out an online application for a job he had been sitting on for quite a while. He kept ruling this job out because he didn't think he could handle the responsibility that came with the position. Out of desperation, he filled out the application and sent it in. Within 30 minutes two women headed to Springfield. They interviewed him for <u>Area Manager for a very large company and hired him on the spot</u>! I knew this was the job that GOD had spoken to me about.

He started this new job immediately but was dealing with such poor eyesight that he was in a constant state of panic, yet had to keep on working. He felt like the world was literally closing in on him as it was the season for the days to get dark earlier and he needed to see to drive. He managed to get an appointment with a very good optometrist who assured him she could get his eyesight back in one eye with cataract surgery. However, she gave him little hope for the other eye that was more problematic.

Prior to the surgery, he was listening to praise tapes on *YouTube* and rolling the lyrics to praise and worship songs over and over in his mind throughout the night. Then one night, he heard the words, "20/20 20/20 Faithful. 20/20 20/20 Faithful. 20/20 20/20 Faithful!" He heard it spoken three times. When God speaks the same thing two or three times, there is more emphasis being put into the message and possibly God's way of getting our undivided attention. I believe what Steve received was a revelatory impartation from heaven's Throne Room! We thought God was revealing to him that **HE** was faithful enough to restore 20/20 vision to him in **both eyes.** He went through the surgery, and two weeks later **TESTED 20/20 VISION IN BOTH EYES! YES, LORD!** Still, today, we give God the Glory!

Yet another physical condition Steve had been dealing with over a rather long period of time had been growing increasingly worse. I've chosen to let him share this with my readers in his own words as follows:

"*Over the past couple of years, I've been tested four times and found to be anemic although I'd not dealt with the issue. Around six months ago, my job became a challenge as I found myself driving several hours each night and working far from home. I became exhausted and weak, and my nerves were frayed. I didn't know how I was going to continue.*

One night I was just starting the long trip home when I remembered Judy telling me about Dr. Sandra Kennedy's[21] statement, 'If GOD thinks I'm healed, and I think I'm sick; then somebody's confused, and it isn't GOD!'

I started loudly praising the FATHER for the sacrifice of His SON for me and for all who believe in Him. I thanked the FATHER for His gift to me and stated over and over that 'I am not confused about my healing!' As I was driving and praying, I suddenly felt as if something 'washed' right through me in a flash! I was wide awake and strong and enthusiastic in that instant! I felt wonderful for the first time in many months!

I immediately called Judy and told her that 'I'm not confused about my healing!' Of course, I then explained to her what had happened. I have since continued on in the same somewhat difficult circumstances, but I've not had that burned out feeling of exhaustion and frayed nerves since! A recent blood test showed no sign of anemia."

---

[21] Dr. Sandra Kennedy: founder and president of *Sandra Kennedy Ministries;* founder and Senior Pastor of *Whole Life Ministries.*

Not only has Steve grown in Biblical understanding of the ways to **appropriate** GOD's promise of physical healing, but he has also gone through much **inner healing**! Whether he realizes this himself or not, others have seen a big difference in the way he has overcome obstacles in the social arena since he has been **thrust** outside his comfort zone. By having to take on unforeseen challenges that have come by way of enormous responsibility, through the **grace** of GOD he has been able to take the bull by the horns and handle every situation with the same self-discipline and work ethic he has always portrayed. Heaven takes notice when we are consistently committed and diligent to stay the course through thick and thin over long periods of time remaining dependent upon the Grace of GOD.

GOD has shown HIMSELF FAITHFUL to Steve time and time again and through it all Steve has learned to put **his trust** in the LORD! Many of you reading this book may recall from our prayer meetings a song that became very popular. Initially released by Andrae Crouch[22], the main lyrics say: "Through it all, through it all, I've learned to trust in JESUS, learned to trust in GOD! Through it all, through it all, I've learned to depend upon HIS WORD!" (*by Andrae Crouch, 1971, Manna Music, Inc.*)

Personal Note: In the Apostle Paul's second letter to Timothy (1:12), he wrote: "*For this reason I also suffer these things, but I am not ashamed; for I know Whom I have believed and I am convinced that He is able to guard what I have entrusted to Him until that day.*" **Yes! GOD IS ABLE!** No matter how tumultuous the winds may get or how dark the clouds may appear as they roll in, we can **see**

---

[22] Andrae Crouch: American Gospel singer, songwriter, and pastor; known as the "father of modern Gospel music."

JESUS with eyes of faith and **know within our spirits** that He is in the boat—our secure place with us—if we have **invited Him in**.

Chapter Seven

People Connections ~ Reconnections

Throughout our daily walk with the LORD, we are given opportunities to exercise our ability to hear His voice as He speaks to us. In doing so, we come to realize that He not only connects us with other people so that we can be of special assistance to them, but in the process we are being helped and encouraged by those same people.

> Psalm 8:3-4 *"When I consider thy heavens, the work of thy fingers, the moon and the stars, which thou hast ordained; what is man that thou art mindful of him? And the son of man, that You visit him?"* (NKJV)

> Also in II Corinthians 1:3-4 *"Blessed be the God and Father of our Lord Jesus Christ, the Father of mercies and God of all comfort, who comforts us in all our affliction so that we will be able to comfort those who are in any affliction with the comfort with which we ourselves are comforted by God."*

Many years ago, one of my closest cousins was battling cancer and it seemed she was on the losing end. Tumors had spread to the base of her brain as the cancer progressed in stages. I was interceding for her in prayer one afternoon; and I heard the LORD say, *"Look into your sister's eyes and call out the spirit of cancer."* I was praying for my cousin, so I thought GOD was telling me that one of my sisters had cancer, as well. I questioned Him about who He was referring to and He said, *"The one who gave you this bedspread."* Then He showed me a vision of the specific bedspread. It was the one I had purchased from the cousin I was praying for.

During this time of prayer, GOD spoke to me using concepts that were different from my immediate thoughts and perceptions. First, He referred to my *cousin* as my **sister.** I quickly understood this *closer relationship* designation because she was a born-again Christian and my *sister-in-the-*LORD! Second, He referred to the bedspread as if she had given it to me when I had actually bought it from her and I still don't know why He did. I had always called it a quilt, not a bedspread. However, even though my mind tried to pick apart the message, THE LORD got His intent through to me.

I made a phone call to my cousin to share with her what I had heard from GOD, because I didn't know when I would be seeing her. She had plans that evening to attend a Bible study at a local Christian bookstore where Pastor Paul Griffis[23] was to be teaching. So I told her to tell Pastor Paul what I heard in my spirit that day while in prayer for her. She did; and he said, "That's from the LORD, and we will do it now!" So he prayed for her and commanded the spirit of cancer to go out in the NAME OF JESUS. **IT DID! Her healing**

---

[23] Paul Griffis: Biblical Advisor and Teacher, *Sounds of Life Foursquare*, Springfield, Illinois.

manifested within two days! Four doctors who had been involved on her case confirmed her healing! **PRAISE THE LORD JESUS CHRIST FOR HIS ULTIMATE MERCY AND GRACE!**

Some weeks later, when my cousin was back to work at *Boys' Club* in Springfield, she called to tell me that a young boy had just told her his family didn't have any food at their house. I was practically out the door myself on the way to the grocery store so I got their address from her. I went to the freezer and loaded up a grocery sack of frozen meat, then picked up a book by Merlin Carothers[24] and put it in the same sack.

This boy and his siblings lived with their mother on the east side of town while I lived ten miles from the west side. I stopped for additional grocery items along the way which caused me to be later than expected, so when I arrived I asked if I could use her phone hoping to confirm my own family-dinner arrangements.

I was still on the phone when she came walking in with the book I had dropped in the meat sack. She proceeded to tell me that she had recently received JESUS as HER SAVIOR in Texas just two months prior to moving to Springfield. There were only two books she had read since her salvation experience; one was the Bible, and the other was the first book Merlin Carothers had written, *"Prison to Praise!"* The book I took to her was Merlin Carothers' second book, *"Power in Praise!"* We both felt it was not a coincidence but God's way of letting her know that the groceries were not from me, they were from

---

[24] Merlin Carothers: Methodist Pastor, author and founder of the **Foundation of Praise**.

GOD Himself and that He **has her back!** Fear gave way to FAITH and a new level of trusting GOD to meet all their everyday needs from that time forward!

What Ever We Have Need Of!

Yes, indeed! Whatever it is we have need of, GOD says He will give it! An African American couple, Douglas and Pamela King, moved to Springfield from St. Louis and they had need of a **church to attend**. They had been praying asking the Lord for His guidance.

As I walked into a local grocery store, I heard GOD say, *"There's someone here I want you to talk to."* By the time I got to the last aisle, I had basically forgotten what He'd said.

I found myself standing next to a woman at the ice cream counter when I heard the Lord say, *"She's the one."* While I stood there wondering what I was supposed to say to her, she walked away. Then, because her friend's daughter wanted ice cream and cake for her birthday, they returned to the ice cream counter. Now that she was back beside me again, I decided to start some kind of dialogue. Anything would do until I figured out what the LORD wanted me to talk to her about. I suggested a certain kind of ice cream to her and she said, "Oh, that does look good." She was curious about the price of the ice cream so we looked for the price together.

I had just had lunch with a friend who had given me $80 in $20 bills so I reached into my wallet and pulled out a $20 bill. I told her a friend had just given me $80, and I thought the LORD wanted me to give her $20 of it. She grabbed the money, held it up in the air, and with eyes as big as saucers shouted, "PRAISE THE LORD!"

Then the other woman who was with her in the store came over. I asked them if they were born-again Christians, baptized in the HOLY GHOST, speaking with other tongues. Both of them were saying, "YES, YES, YES! HALLELUJAH!" They weren't being quiet about it! In fact, it was with raised voices that we all three had a little *praise* and *worship* session right there in the aisle of the grocery store!

I felt an instant kinship with these ladies and asked them where they were going to church. By then, Pam had introduced herself and told me that she and her husband, Doug, along with their daughter, had just moved here from St. Louis. She said they had been praying about a church to go to here. In St. Louis, they attended *Grace World Outreach Center*[25]. In fact, they were part of a cell group there that was also praying for them to find the right church here in Springfield.

I told her that my husband and I had visited their church. We had heard Marilyn Hickey[26], Lester Sumrall[27], T. L. Osborn[28], and several other great speakers at their church. **As the LORD knew**, we *happened* to be attending a church in Springfield with a pastor who had been **working closely with their St. Louis pastor.** So, I invited them to come for a visit. They did, and stayed there for eight years!

---

[25] *Grace World Outreach Center*: Now *GRACE CHURCH* founded by Pastor Ron Tucker.
[26] Marilyn Hickey: Co-founder of *Orchard Road Christian Center*; International Bible teacher called to "cover the earth with God's Word."
[27] Lester Sumrall: founder of LeSEA, producer of magazines, books, study guides, television and radio stations.
[28] T. L. Osborn: world missionary evangelist, statesman, teacher, author; known for his mass-miracle ministry to millions of unreached people in over 90 nations.

Approximately twenty years later, a man came from St. Louis to install a new floor in my kitchen. The process was going to take three days, so I thought if he is going to be in my home for that length of time, I needed to find out where he was spiritually. When he mentioned he was from St. Louis, I told him I had only one St. Louis story. I shared all the details telling him about the time when the LORD spoke to me on my way into the grocery store, and how I ended up talking with this woman in the last aisle of the store. I told him she and her family had been going to *Grace World Outreach Center* in St. Louis and had moved to Springfield and how they had prayed for the Lord to show them which church to go to.

He said, "**Grace Church? That's <u>my</u> church!**"

While I considered how many churches there might be in St. Louis, I thought it might be a different church. After all, he said "Grace Church." He didn't say, "Grace World Outreach Center." So I asked him about his pastor, and yes it was the same pastor who he said he had known for many years!

What were the chances? If God has an anointed message going out to the body in one church and we aren't there to hear it, <u>God can use any means</u> to get the message to us if it's a Word He wants us to hear. So that set the stage for three days of periodic God-centered conversations. We shared Scripture from the Word of GOD and what we felt God's plans were for us, individually, as well as God's move in the corporate Church. God is not only speaking to us through others, but He is speaking to others through us. He knows just what block needs to go into our spiritual houses. His Voice has great power to bring us out of our past difficulties and set us on the course that He has ordained for our future lives. I believe this 3-day exchange of dialogue proved to serve a purpose that was in the mind of God for us at that time. **God is more than a theology**. He is a personal God who cares more about the things that concern us than we even care about them ourselves.

The Wind of the Spirit

I have always been amazed by how the HOLY SPIRIT brings people into my life in ways that grow me in my personal relationship with the LORD! My family is an amazing example.

Many decades ago the Word of God was spreading across this nation and around the world, ignited by *fresh fire*. It was a revival of God's Truth that there is indeed such a thing as the *Baptism of the HOLY SPIRIT* for believers in our day. I first heard about it when a woman in my neighborhood brought me two books. She told me the HOLY SPIRIT was leading her to bring them—to me. One was titled, "*I Believe in Miracles*," by Kathryn Kuhlman[29]; and the other was, "*They Speak With Other Tongues*," by John Sherrell[30].

I didn't read either of these books right away, but remember feeling drawn to them because she said the HOLY SPIRIT led her to bring them to me. When I finally decided to read, "*They Speak With Other Tongues*," and saw where the miracles of healing were meant to continue on into our present day, I thought, **"This is too good to be true!"** Thus began an 8-hour-a-day searching into the Word of God.

My knowledge about the Holy Spirit (and the *Baptism of the Holy Spirit*) was quite limited at that time. However, there were *rumblings* of His active presence throughout my family. It was already

---

[29] Kathryn Kuhlman: One of the most well-known healing ministers and leader in Pentecostalism in the world.
[30] John Sherrell: Author and founder the publishing company, **Chosen Books**, dedicated to developing new Christian writers.

being rumored that something had *happened* to Aunt Dort in Arizona! Relatives were complaining that all she wrote to them about was Jesus. She had become a JESUS FANATIC in her 80's! However, <u>prior</u> to her receiving the *Baptism of the HOLY SPIRIT*, she was writing to us **–with distinct disapproval**—about what JESUS FANATICS her grandchildren had become! This was happening between the years 1970-1975 that we began to hear all the buzz. There was something in the air, and it was blowing profusely!

While I was still trying to figure out what was happening with my relatives, I wrote to Aunt Dort asking her what she believed about the Baptism of the Holy Spirit. Prior to mailing the letter, I stopped by my sister's house and saw where Aunt Dort had sent a booklet to her with the title, "*Have You Received the Baptism of the Holy Spirit?*" I then added a note to the letter I had just written to Aunt Dort telling her to disregard the question I had asked about the Baptism of the Holy Spirit because I had seen the booklet she sent to Janice.

Soon after, our <u>mother</u> began a hot pursuit to know JESUS more. It wasn't long before she was delving into the Word of God herself and sending for teaching material through Kenneth and Gloria Copeland[31]. She was putting everything she was learning into practice.

When she was in a lot of pain and her doctor was telling her the only thing that would give her relief would be for her to undergo surgery, she wouldn't have it. I had taken her to her appointment that day. When we arrived back at her house, she sat down at the kitchen table and told me she was too old for surgery. Then she shook her hand at me across the table and made this bold statement. "My

---

[31] Kenneth and Gloria Copeland: Founders of *Kenneth Copeland Ministries*; leaders of the Charismatic Movement, speakers and televangelists.

JESUS is going to heal me!" She threw her pain medication in the garbage can, and **the pain went with it!**

When our other aunt started attending the Pentecostal church in her town, both her daughters started attending church with her and they all began to experience a more personal walk with the Lord.

My husband, Gerald, had prayed the prayer of Salvation (asking for forgiveness of sin and inviting Jesus into his heart) with our pastor in the Baptist church we had attended, and now ten years later he also prayed to receive the *Baptism of the Holy Spirit*. One of the first books he read was titled, "*Mr. Pentecost*," by David Du Plessis[32]. Smith Wigglesworth[33] had prophesied to Du Plessis in 1936 that he was going to step over into stronger things and deeper things than he had ever thought was possible and that God was going to use him to bring a renewed knowledge of Pentecostal power to the Catholic Church and the old-line denominational churches. By the 1950's God had begun to open doors for Du Plessis and in the mid 1970's we were just beginning to hear about it!

Aunt Dort's grandchildren, Ronnie and Connie (who are brother and sister) received Salvation and the Baptism of the HOLY SPIRIT nearly the same time; Connie in 1971, and Ron in 1972. Their grandmother, our Aunt Dort, received JESUS as her personal Savior and Baptizer in the HOLY SPIRIT around 1975 and her husband (Pop to all of us) several years later. Aunt Dort and Pop have gone on to be with JESUS in Heaven while Ronnie and Connie have continued in the ways of the LORD in all these years and remained active in

---

[32] David Du Plessis: South African-born Pentecostal minister considered one of the main founders of the charismatic movement.
[33] Smith Wigglesworth: British Evangelist and Faith Healer often referred to as "the Apostle of Faith."

full Gospel churches no matter where they have lived. Ron and his wife, Pam, are presently residing in Colorado where Ron is involved in a prison ministry. Connie and her husband, Keith, are living in Minnesota.

<u>Timely Visit</u>

Last summer, these cousins stayed with me when they brought their mother here to visit her sisters. One of the things we love to share are the many ways that the HOLY SPIRIT teaches us from the Word of GOD and the various ways that He communicates the truths of God's Word to us. During this visit, Ron shared how the HOLY SPIRT brought some very important insights to light in his life when he and Pam lived in the mountains outside Santa Fe, New Mexico. He has given me permission to share this story with you who happen to be reading my book. In fact, he has even given it a title:

"Ruts & The Kingdom of Self."

"The last hill on the road that led to our driveway had a lot of gray clay in it and when the first snows melted that portion of the road turned extremely miry. The very first time I drove up the hill in my four-wheel drive truck, I made deep ruts all the way to the top. Subsequently, every time I drove up that hill my truck tires automatically dropped into those ruts with no way out. As long as I kept my foot lightly on the gas pedal, the truck easily moved forward.

It was here that the Lord showed me that I had not been letting issues go...taking offense...being annoyed...and falling over and over again into the same old rut. There are a number of kingdom strongholds out here, and one is the Kingdom of Self."

This illustration from my cousin, Ron, was brought to my attention at a very good time because GOD is showing me that He wants to restore the Church to the *ways* He communicated with the early Church—and Ron's testimony is a great example. God's *still small voice*, angels speaking, and the HOLY SPIRIT directing are avenues by which revelatory impartations—through fasting and praying on the part of the believers—are received.

> Romans 8:5,6 tells us, *"For those who are according to the flesh set their minds on the things of the flesh, but those who are according to the Spirit, the things of the Spirit. For the mind set on the flesh is death, but the mind set on the Spirit is life and peace."*

When I listened to Ron, I could see and *feel* his experience which in turn allowed the Holy Spirit to show me more of the concepts He wanted me to understand. God had been showing me HOW MUCH He wants to RESTORE His Church to its <u>authentic purpose</u>. And yet, His people are "bogged down" in the ruts of human traditions, distracting them and causing them to fall deeper into enemy strongholds. God is the **Breaker** of strongholds—human or otherwise—and He desires that we become acutely aware of the *ruts* that hold us in positions counter to His Ways. Only then will we be able to FULLY hear His *still small voice*—to cooperate with His ministering angels—to accept the guidance of the Holy Spirit and to allow <u>all</u> our steps to be directed by His Grace, Mercy and Power.

GOD is greater than anything the world might deal out to you or me. GOD is saying to the world with its many crises, *"When you bring US your worst, WE are going to give you our best!"* GOD has a way out of every situation that has kept us bound. We can be at peace no matter what **season** we are going through. A changed life that exemplifies an inner transformation to all who witness it can be a sign and a wonder within itself, even when the work is an inward accomplishment involving angelic forces. The devil has no choice but to cease and give up in the Name of JESUS. However, we still have to fight and do our part to accomplish this! All our sins were placed on JESUS and our redemption is being manifested through a purging process. Knowing everything about us, GOD sent His SON, JESUS, to stand in the gap for us—**become sin**—so that we will not receive the punishment we deserve (Romans 5:6 and 8 and Romans 6:23).

> Before we were born, God knew us and **set us apart**. Jeremiah 1:5, *"Before I formed you in the womb I knew you, and before you were born I consecrated you; I have appointed you a prophet to the nations."*

> Then in Romans 1:1-7 the Apostle Paul wrote, *"Paul, a bond-servant of Christ Jesus, called as an apostle,,* **set apart for the Gospel of God**, *which He promised beforehand through His prophets in the holy Scriptures, concerning His Son, who was born a descendant of David according to the flesh, who was declared the Son of God with power by the resurrection from the dead, according to the Spirit of holiness, Jesus Christ our Lord, through whom we have received grace and apostleship to bring about the obedience of faith among all the Gentiles for His name's sake, among whom* **you also are the called of**

Jesus Christ; to all who are beloved of God in Rome, ***called as saints****: Grace to you and peace from God our Father and the Lord Jesus Christ."*

Our separation from the world as Christians is measured by the same degree as the Word of God within us is being spoken through us. We are continually being moved into our *New Day* of many wonderful things happening, but there are things from our past that we can't take with us. Jesus' death, burial, and resurrection work in us so that JESUS' life can flow through us to others. This process is called ***sanctification*** which is a supernatural work that is going on in us while we remain on this earth—all the rest of our days—for His Kingdom Purposes. Yet, at the same time we must see our sanctification as a finished work of the Cross. **We are becoming what we have already been made to be through Christ's death, burial, and resurrection**—through His impartations of truth that are continually being revealed to us line upon line, precept upon precept.

Persecution and trial is how this death and renewal process is accomplished. Many of us will feel like we've walked through hell in order for JESUS to complete the sanctification process within us. **His Life**—Jesus' Way to help and support us—is His Word that we speak into our life's situations. It is during the **heat** of trials where we are more apt to look for the Lord's willingness to save us, most often after we've exhausted every means of the flesh or every avenue within this worldly system that is made available to us.

Jesus' Life is His Word that we also speak into situations where others are concerned even if they don't think they want to hear it. We must die to the flesh ourselves or we will be hesitant to speak what

God's Word says to others. We will be more interested in avoiding persecution and protecting our reputation, especially among our peers.

What is it we are called to? We are called to be **ambassadors** for Christ! Ambassadors who are ready, willing, and able—available to carry God's presence to those who need to encounter Him. In II Corinthians 7:8-12, there are specific <u>attitudes</u> brought to light in the Apostle Paul's letter to the Corinthian Church that will help us today.

> *"For though I caused you sorrow by my letter, I do not regret it; though I did regret it—for I see that that letter caused you sorrow, though only for a while. I now rejoice, not that you were made sorrowful, but that you were made sorrowful to the point of repentance; for you were made sorrowful according to the will of God, so that you might not suffer loss in anything through us. For the sorrow that is according to the will of God produces a repentance without regret, leading to salvation, but the sorrow of the world produces death. For behold what earnestness this very thing, this godly sorrow, has produced in you: what vindication of yourselves, what indignation, what fear, what longing, what zeal, what avenging of wrong! In everything you demonstrated yourselves to be innocent in the matter. So although I wrote to you, it was not for the sake of the offender nor for the sake of the one offended, but that your earnestness on our behalf might be made known to you in the sight of God."*

Because it is at the point of repentance that we begin our *sanctification* process, I've gleaned much from the following quote by David Wilkerson—January 5, 2007—writing about repentance in his WORLD CHALLENGE Pulpit series:

> "To repent is to experience such contrition as to change one's way of life. Simply put, repentance is turning from one's sin and going in the opposite direction.
>
> Repentance is not meritorious. Only the sacrifice of Christ's blood can forgive. But repentance is the only way to know true healing and rejoicing. There is no other way to enter the peace and rest of Christ except through the doors of repentance.
>
> Let me give you the background of Paul's letter to the Corinthians. He had exposed the sin of incest in their congregation, but nobody dealt with it. And because this awful sin was overlooked, there was no remorse among the people.
>
> So Paul wrote the church an even stronger message. Now, as the people sat listening to his letter read aloud in the congregation, they were pricked at heart. And they repented, full of godly sorrow at not having faced the exceeding sin in their midst. That repentance brought great rejoicing.

> Now Paul encouraged them, saying, *'See what godly sorrow did for you? It wrought a carefulness in you. It brought an indignation against your own sin.'* Repentance is the only way healing and strength can come to those who are caught up in sin.
>
> Repentance and trust in Christ's redeeming blood result in total remission of sin, and that means pardon, forgiveness and freedom from sin's power. According to Paul, there can be no conversion, no freedom, no born-again miracle without repentance: *"Repent ye therefore, and be converted, that your sins may be blotted out, when the times of refreshing shall come from the presence of the Lord."* (Acts 3:19).

If Godly repentance for the early Church can make a way for such a <u>carefulness</u> to be wrought in them—such clearing, vehement desire, and zeal—then those of us today have the opportunity to follow after this same example of ***caring* for one another**. How we relate to Christ's death, burial, and resurrection EXPERIENCIALLY is covered in depth and detail throughout Watchman Nee's[34] three-volume series titled, *"The Spiritual Man."*

The rate at which we mature in the Kingdom of GOD relates to how much we are going to believe for Godly Wisdom which comes

---

[34] Watchman Nee: Called to be a *watchman* raised up to sound out a warning call in the dark night to deliver people from the tyranny of *self-life*.

through impartations of revelation from His Word. The devil knows that he doesn't have to give up unless he is discovered and faced down. So, again I say, we must stand our ground and fight for this. As we war in the spirit by sending Scriptures into situations and circumstances, we are shown things that the devil does not want us to see. GOD is saying, "**Enough is enough!**" Enemy forces have been holding the Church back long enough! The attacks against our lives have <u>not</u> been because of our past; the attacks have been because of **the <u>future</u> GOD has planned for us**!

When writing this book, I heard in my spirit—by way of a vision with words—a command to move three older airplanes out of a hangar because three new jet planes were on their way here and *already in the air!* Then I saw what looked like a passenger jet that was bright shiny gold as the sun reflected on it! As I prayed, I came to believe these spiritual jets are coming for the believers who GOD is about to raise up to impact society in this next outpouring of His HOLY SPIRIT!

A few days later, I crossed paths with one such woman who I believe GOD is going to use mightily in this next great *outpouring of His Spirit!* Several years ago, I received a prophetic word concerning her. What I heard in my spirit was that **she is more than a friend, but one in whom GOD has wrought a work in, and that she is to be counted among those of the evening and the morning of the Third Day!** Anne and I both wondered how close we are getting to seeing the same **resurrection power that raised JESUS from the dead** manifesting in our own lives and the lives of those who we are coming in contact with. We have both been sensing we were getting very close! We are moving into a day when we are going to see with eyes of faith that all of our petitions have been granted! God is saying, *"Ask me whatever you want; I will give it thee!"* All that we need, He has already provided! **Great and awesome victories are forthcoming!**

On that day, prior to seeing this friend, I was sitting at a traffic light and noticed a paving truck next to me. The company name on this truck may as well have been GOD & SONS PAVING for within the actual name was one of the attributes of GOD HIMSELF—MERCIFUL!

Later in the afternoon, I was reading an article online from one of God's prophets titled, "GOD IS PAVING NEW ROAD WAYS."

Then later I was being shown (in one separate vision) three new roads with fresh ASPHALT PAVEMENT. On top of fresh asphalt were **large white letters** in all caps spelling out these words lengthwise: "LONGEVITY," "RAPID ADVANCEMENT," and "MYSTERIES REVEALED." This vision strengthened the foundation of God's Word (His Truths in Scripture) in my heart, while at the same time, allowed me to know where He is taking me.

Some Christian believers only share what they know with other people who already know the same things. However, I was shown another vision of a robin leaping from one branch to a higher branch and heard in my spirit, *"It is GOD's season to spring forth with **new things** being shared—things that others **do not** already know about!"*

We must bear in mind that the things the HOLY SPIRIT wants us to share with others—His revelation gifts—are derived from the things that GOD has already wrought in us or revealed to us. When we follow His direction and share these things, we can expect numerous responses. If I were to give a friend a special gift that no appreciation was shown toward, that would only involve a personal gift from me in the natural sense of the word. However, when we are operating through the *Gifts of the HOLY SPIRIT*, then any rejection of what we give/share would be against the **person of the HOLY SPIRIT!**

An analogy to this could be illustrated through a dream I had about a year ago. In the dream, I drove up to a 3-way intersection on a country road and saw a white **LOVE SEAT** with off white stripes that was the matching piece to my own living room set. I had given the love seat to someone, and they had discarded it at this intersection. It was sitting there dumped by the side of the road waiting for whoever might want it to pick up. I decided to take it back home with me to protect it from the elements until I found someone else who might want it.

An expected, common response to sharing this dream with another Christian might be that I had *cast my pearls before swine* in this situation, whatever situation the dream might have been referring to. The Word of GOD says in Matthew 7:6...

> *"Do not give what is holy to dogs, and do not throw your pearls before swine, lest they trample them under their feet, and turn and tear you to pieces."*

However, we can be encouraged to follow the Holy Spirit's guidance to share what He's showing us because the Word says in I Corinthians 3:7...

> *"So then neither the one who plants nor the one who waters is anything, but GOD who causes the growth."*

Paul also said in I Corinthians 4:3-5..."*But to me it is a very small thing that I may be examined by you, or by any human court; in fact, I do not even examine myself. For I am conscious of nothing against myself, yet I am not by this acquitted; but the one who examines me is the Lord. Therefore do not go on passing judgment before the time, but wait until the Lord comes who will both bring to light the things hidden in the darkness and disclose the motives of men's hearts; and then each man's praise will come to him from God."*

If people reject what we share with them, we can stand in the gap for them and intercede for them in prayer, but <u>we don't have to beat ourselves up over it</u>. When the Bible speaks of unbelief, didn't those people have to have something presented to them for them to be in disbelief over? The most important thing for us is to remain in **LOVE** toward everyone involved!

GOD is releasing **new power** for us to complete our destinies. We must go through the fire and come out on the other side if we are to impact society with **God's LOVE!** He chooses us out of the fire!

Angels Among Us

Angels are involved in this process—this transformation—that is taking us deeper in revelation of God's Word and lifting us **higher in Him** than we have ever been before! GOD by His wisdom, grace, and mercy is equipping the saints with greater power and new warfare strategies. The Army of the LORD—including Angels and Saints in heaven and on earth—is being enabled to take more territory for His Kingdom by more and more people receiving salvation, healing, and deliverance. The enemy forces are being weakened because of new

Divine revelation which is being imparted to the saints. **Hallelujah! God is raising up a people, and strongholds are coming down! Strongholds of fear, strongholds of doubt, and strongholds of religiosity are crumbling.**

God is saying, *"Rise up with faith and holiness; preach the Word and shake that which cannot be shaken. Some will feel the fire in their bones, and others will order you out of their houses."*

No matter where we are in our individual experiences in knowing and growing in Christ Jesus, the HOLY SPIRIT can reveal this to us <u>as we go</u>. We each need to have some idea of where we are in our spiritual growth process and where we fit in with the Body of Christ at any given time. We can be in the valley, or we can be on the mountaintop, or we can be anywhere in between at any given time.

In the year 2000, I woke up from a dream where I was riding in a car with a woman friend on a mountain road. We had no idea how far we had come up this mountain until we were looking out across the terrain at the **very tops of thousands of huge tall cedar trees!** I thought that was an interesting dream!

Then, that very night, Thomas Kinkade[35] was a guest on TBN (*Trinity Broadcasting Network*). They were featuring the unveiling of his latest painting called, *"Sunrise."* As the veil was being removed, you could see that it was a huge rock with a wooden cross on top of the rock, and Thomas Kinkade was explaining how he wanted everything in this painting to **depict height!** For this very reason, he chose to go off to the side of the rock and paint **just the tops of three cedar trees!**

---

[35] Thomas Kinkade: known as "The Painter of Light" gained his inspiration from his religious beliefs hoping to touch people of all faiths.

The HOLY SPIRIT does not leave us alone to guess where we are in our ascent to higher ground. Nor does He leave us there—on those high and successful peaks—because it is in the *valley experiences* where we learn to put more and more of our trust in Him! It is GOD who makes our feet *like hinds' feet* and causes us to walk upon our high places. He is GOD of **both**, the mountains and the valleys. He is also GOD of the deserts, foothills, plains, pastures, and plateaus. THERE IS NO PLACE IN THE HEAVENS, ON EARTH, OR UNDER THE EARTH that we can go, that HE is not THERE WITH US.

Personal Note: Going back to cousin Ron's revelatory dissertation regarding the ruts from heavy rains along the foothills outside of Santa Fe—When GOD begins to pour out **His Spirit** on us in greater measure, we are shown the things He is rescuing us from <u>before</u> He ROLLS us into our NEXT SEASON!

AND, like the *hind* (the female deer remarkable for fleetness or swiftness that God made able to climb great heights as well as traverse the valleys and escape fast-running foes), He has given us uniquely individual gifts that will enable us to accomplish His Purposes for us. Another attribute of the *hind* is that her front hooves have the ability to <u>search</u> for the rocks that have <u>a solid foundation</u> under them and are not as apt to shift from the weight of her body when she brings her back hooves forward onto that same solid footing while climbing on more rugged terrain.

ON EVERY LEVEL, GOD has and IS preparing us and protecting us. So let it rain, let it rain, let it rain to the extent that none of us remain exempt from this process!

Chapter Eight

Our Covenant of Faith

Growing up in the country as a 17 year-old and searching for a summer project to occupy my spare time, I decided to take a correspondence course through the mail on the Bible. When I came to the story of JESUS speaking with Nicodemus and telling him that unless one is *born again* he cannot see the Kingdom of God, I realized that I'd never learned what being "born again" meant. If Jesus placed such value upon it with Nicodemus, then I needed to know more.

That afternoon, I decided to go to my bedroom and pray to God until I felt positive that I had been *born again*. Knowing <u>nothing</u> about *how* to do this, having <u>never</u> been in a church where any kind of invitation had been given to come forward and accept Jesus as my Lord and Savior, or <u>ever</u> hearing anyone explain this concept to me, one might say I was being made aware of the fact that <u>there are things in this life that are worth seeking</u>. I didn't know if I could be *born again* in an instant or if it might take days, weeks, or months. All I knew was that I wasn't coming out of my bedroom until I knew beyond a shadow of a doubt that I had been *born again*!

No sooner had I begun to pray to God about this when I felt **a spiritual cleansing** that went all over me reaching even to the tips of my fingers! Suddenly, <u>I knew</u> that Heaven was a real place where our prayers are not only heard but answered! Thus, began my Christian Journey.

The Apostle Paul was inspired to write in his letter to the Galatians (3:16-29) that…

> *"Now the promises were spoken to Abraham and to his seed. He does not say, 'And to seeds,' as referring to many, but rather to one, 'And to your seed,' that is, Christ. What I am saying is this: the Law, which came four hundred and thirty years later,* ***does not invalidate a covenant previously ratified by God****, so as to nullify the promise. For if the inheritance is based on law, it is no longer based on a promise; but God has granted it to Abraham by means of a promise.*
>
> *Why the Law then? It was added because of transgressions, having been ordained through angels by the agency of a mediator,* ***until the seed would come*** *to whom the promise had been made. Now a mediator is not for one party only; whereas God is only one. Is the Law then contrary to the promises of God? May it never be! For if a law had been given which was able to impart life, then righteousness would indeed have been based on law. But the Scripture has shut up everyone under sin,* ***so that the promise by faith in Jesus Christ might be given to those who believe****.*

But before faith came, we were kept in custody under the law, being shut up to the faith which was later to be revealed. Therefore, **the Law has become our tutor to lead us to Christ, so that we may be justified by faith.** *But now that faith has come, we are no longer under a tutor. For you are all sons of God through faith in Christ Jesus. For all of you who were baptized into Christ have clothed yourselves with Christ. There is neither Jew nor Greek, there is neither slave nor free man, there is neither male nor female; for you are all one in Christ Jesus. And if you belong to Christ, then you are Abraham's descendants, heirs according to promise."*

We all enter into this covenant through Jesus Christ when we invite Him into our lives. It is <u>with</u> Christ, <u>through</u> the shedding of His Blood on the Cross of Calvary where His Suffering and Death—in our place—made a way for us to receive forgiveness for our sins.

Even though what I've shared above <u>how I *felt* a spiritual cleansing</u> sweep over me at the time I prayed to be *born again*, <u>it is just as likely</u> that people will not feel anything happening in that moment in time. When people pray to receive Christ into their life and be born again, they ask this of God strictly by faith. **Everyone's *born again experience* is unique to that individual.**

If you are reading this book now and have never asked JESUS into your life—never asked Him to save you and bring you into *family relationship* with Him—you are welcome to use the following as a guide. **More importantly, whatever words you choose to use, let this be a prayer from your heart:**

Father God, I believe that You have a plan for my life that I can enter into by the mercy and grace that You have provided for me through the sacrifice of your Son, Jesus.

I ask you, Jesus, to forgive me of my sins. I invite You to come into my life so that I can come to know You personally as my Lord and Savior from this day forth. I pray that my name be written down in Your Lamb's Book of Life so that I can spend eternity with You in heaven.

I believe that You hear my prayer because I call upon You according to Your Word that You will come into my heart and make me a new creation fashioned after Your will for my life.

I give you thanks, Father God, for saving me and coming into my life as You promised before the foundation of the world that whosoever calls upon You shall be saved. Amen!

All of heaven rejoices at the moment every man, woman, and child comes into the Family of God! At the point of salvation—our adoption as God's own son or daughter—our names are written down in the *LAMB'S BOOK of LIFE* for ALL ETERNITY! According to Ephesians 1:11-13, we learn that...

"....we have obtained an inheritance..." "...to the end that we who were the first to hope in Christ would be to the praise of His glory. In Him, you also, after listening to the message of truth, the Gospel of your salvation—having also believed, you were SEALED in Him with the Holy Spirit of promise...."

Also as it is written in Titus 3:5-7: **"He saved us**, *not on the basis of deeds which we have done in righteousness,* **but according to His mercy, by the washing of regeneration and renewing by the Holy Spirit**, *whom He poured out upon us richly through Jesus Christ our Savior, so that* **being justified by His grace** *we would be made heirs according to the hope of eternal life."*

Regarding our new <u>position</u> in God's family, we might desire to follow through with **water baptism** according to the same pattern or doctrine as Jesus when He was baptized by John—as were all the disciples of His day—as well as the days that followed after His ascension back to the Father.

Romans 6:3-5 says, *"Do you not know that all of us who have been baptized into Christ Jesus have been baptized into His death? Therefore, we have been buried with Him through baptism into death,*

> *so that as Christ was raised from the dead through the glory of the Father, so **we too might walk in newness of life**."*

Water Baptism announces to the world that we believe in and accept Jesus as our Lord and Savior and are **obedient to His command**. Matthew 28:19-20...

> *"Go therefore and make disciples of all the nations, **baptizing them** in the name of the Father and the Son and the Holy Spirit, teaching them to observe all that I commanded you; and lo, I am with you always, even to the end of the age."*

Water Baptism also demonstrates that we follow Jesus' personal example to be baptized: Luke 3:21-22...

> *"Now when **all the people were baptized, Jesus was also baptized**, and while He was praying, heaven was opened, and the Holy Spirit descended upon Him in bodily form like a dove, and a voice came out of heaven, 'You are My beloved Son, in You I am well-pleased."*

Also...the Baptism of the Holy Spirit—The Third Person of the Trinity—empowers us to **more fully** *live* our new lives: Acts 2:38-39...

> *"Peter said to them, 'Repent, and each of you **baptized** in the name of Jesus Christ for the forgiveness of your sins; and you will **receive the gift of the Holy Spirit**. For the promise is for <u>you and your children</u> and for <u>all</u> who are far off, as many as the Lord our God will call to Himself.'"*

Throughout the Book of Acts, we are shown examples of how we are to **act**. We are given many accounts of the believers going out with *power* doing **the same works** that JESUS did when HE walked among them! JESUS COMMANDED THEM (in the first chapter of Acts 1:4) to *wait for the Promise of the Father* which, He said, *"You heard of from me."* He had already spoken to them about the need to receive the BAPTISM OF—FELLOWSHIP OF—POWER OF—THE HOLY SPIRIT!

> In John 7:38-39: *"He who believes in Me, as the Scripture said, 'From his innermost being will flow rivers of living water.' But <u>this He spoke of the Spirit</u>, whom those who believed in Him were to receive;* ***for the Spirit was not yet given, because Jesus was not yet glorified.***"

> In John 14:16,17: *"I will ask the Father, and He will give you another Helper, that He may be with you forever; that is the Spirit of truth, whom the world*

cannot receive, because it does not see Him or know Him, but you know Him because **He abides with you and will be in you.**"

Acts 2:33: *"Therefore having been exalted to the right hand of God, and having received from the Father the promise of the Holy Spirit, He has poured forth this* **which you both see and hear."**

JESUS has already told them <u>how the Holy Spirit will work within them</u> in John 14:12…

"Truly, truly, I say to you, he who believes in Me, **the works that I do, he will do also;** *and greater works than these he will do; because I go to the Father."*

Also, in Mark 16:15-18: *"And He said to them, 'Go into all the world and preach the Gospel to all creation. He who has believed and has been baptized shall be saved; but he who has disbelieved shall be condemned.* **These signs will accompany those who have believed**: *in My name they will cast out demons, they will speak with new tongues; they will pick up serpents, and if they drink any deadly poison, it will not hurt them; they will lay hands on the sick, and they will recover.'"*

All throughout the Book of Acts, we see where *speaking with other tongues* was the initial evidence of their receiving the Baptism of the HOLY SPIRIT and **the laying on of hands** was the most common way of praying for this endowment of power to transfer to others. One example can be found in the 19th Chapter of Acts when the Apostle Paul came upon believers in Ephesus. He asked them, "Have you received the Holy Ghost since you believed?" Because they knew ONLY of water baptism, Paul laid his hands on them and the Holy Ghost came on them—empowering them further to speak with tongues and prophesy.

As long as the devil is still putting sicknesses, diseases, and infirmities on people we—as believers—need this power of the Holy Spirit to command the evil spirits out and heal the sick by the authority that is invested in us to use JESUS' NAME! Are not we, you and I who are involved in taking new territory for the KINGDOM OF GOD, a part of this same COVENANT OF FAITH as the early Church? Do we not have the same Holy Spirit enabling us to participate with like initiative in our time as they did theirs?

The Word of God tells us that the world is at enmity with GOD (James 4:4). If we need to wonder how much at enmity this world is that we live in today we can examine the account of the Apostle Paul when he was at sea with 276 men in all, mostly prisoners as was he. (Acts 27:1-44). As they came to the place called the fair havens, nigh unto the city of Lasea, the Bible says that sailing had become even more dangerous because the time of their **fasting** had passed! Evidently, it was their *fasting* that had been holding back the **winds of adversity**! At that point, Paul admonished them saying: *"Men, I perceive that the voyage will certainly be attended with damage and* *great loss, not only of the cargo and the ship, but also of our lives."* (Acts 27:10)

They paid no attention to Paul but decided to sail on anyway. Then there arose another **tempestuous** wind called Euroclydon—a violent hurricane-force wind—by which they were even more exceedingly tossed about to the point that they lost all hope!

Paul was in prayer again until an angel appeared to him and assured him that none of their lives would be lost, only the destruction of the ship. Not only was Paul fasting and praying; but even after that, it states in the Word that the rest of the men had been **fasting** for <u>fourteen days</u>. (Acts 27:33)

I have my own theory here which is that during that extended length of time when Paul was praying in the ship away from all the rest of them, he was getting very **prayed up!** I am basing this on the fact that not only did an **angel** appear to him assuring him that there would be no loss of life, but after they managed to get to shore, he was able to shake off a "**venomous**" beast that had bitten him on the hand. (Acts 28:3-5) I am convinced that the time Paul spent in prayer, spiritual **warfare** was being engaged (he went down in the ship to fight) which made way for a powerful breakthrough that launched him into ***Faith*** for his next series—or season—of miracles. Not only were all the men saved, Paul was able to shake off the venomous beast without feeling any harm, and he went on from there to heal the father of the chief man of that island along with many others who went to him to be healed.

Additionally, I believe that much of Paul's praying was done **in the spirit** because Paul is the one who claimed to speak in tongues more than anyone and "would that **all spoke in tongues**" (I Corinthians 14:5). When he prayed in the spirit, his own understanding was unfruitful so he would do both. He prayed with the spirit, and he prayed with the understanding. He not only sang with the spirit, but he also sang with the understanding! (I Corinthians 14:14-15) He also THANKED GOD FOR IT, THIS ABILITY TO PRAY CONCERNING SITUATIONS THE WAY THE HOLY SPIRIT SEES FIT!

The Word isn't clear exactly when Paul received his prayer language even though the Word is clear when many of the others did. It does, however, give the account of when Paul received the <u>infilling of the HOLY SPIRIT</u> by the laying on of hands by Ananias in Acts 9:17 which is when most are convinced he received his prayer language. The logical conclusion is that Paul started speaking in tongues when he was filled with the Holy Ghost just as many of the believers did in so many other accounts.

What about you and me? In Luke 11:9-13, JESUS says...

> *"So I say to you, ask, and it will be given to you; seek, and you will find; knock, and it will be opened to you. For everyone who asks, receives; and he who seeks, finds; and to him who knocks, it will be opened. Now suppose one of you fathers is asked by his son for a fish; he will not give him a snake instead of a fish, will he? Or if he is asked for an egg, he will not give him a scorpion, will he? If you then, being evil, know how to give good gifts to your children,* **how much more will your heavenly Father give the Holy Spirit to those who ask Him?"**

In Scripture, every place where the HOLY SPIRIT was at work _**among**_ the people, we see the **supernatural power of GOD** at work _**in the lives**_ of the people. On the Day of Pentecost when Peter stood up in the midst of everyone present (Acts 2:14-36), he was inspired to remind them of the Prophet Joel's words concerning the outpouring of the Holy Spirit: "..._your sons and your daughters will prophesy, and your young men will see visions, and your old men will dream dreams._" Peter's words prepared them to open their hearts and minds to all that the LORD made available to them.

> In Acts 16:9-10, it says: "_A vision appeared to Paul in the night: a man of Macedonia was standing and appealing to him and saying, '**Come over to Macedonia and help us**.' When he had seen the vision, immediately we sought to go into Macedonia, concluding that God had called us to preach the Gospel to them._"

Indeed, from the moment of Paul's meeting with the Lord, Jesus, on that road to Damascus, and throughout the rest of his earthly life, Paul relied on the visions and dreams sent to him by the Holy Spirit.

Here we see where a vision appeared to Paul in the night, and those who were with him were equally accepting of the fact that these were instructions being sent to—not only Paul—but all the men who were ministering with him. They consented in one accord that God had called **them** to preach the Gospel in Macedonia.

This might be a place—in reading this book—where each of us could pull back and examine our own walk with the Lord. What if only one within a group of us were to report seeing a similar type vision? Would we be this eager to comply—**to act immediately**—if the vision was given to only one person and no one else in the group? Yet, without hesitation, those people who accompanied Paul <u>all</u> went!

All throughout the New Testament, Apostles, disciples, and believers (like you and me) were led by visions, dreams, angelic visitations, and the Holy Spirit speaking to them, directing them, and admonishing them. **There was never a dull moment!!**

Another example is when Paul and Silas prayed and sang praises unto God from within a dark and murky dungeon, and suddenly there was a great earthquake! The foundations of the prison were shaken, the doors were opened, and their shackles all came loose! (Acts 16:25-28)

Today, we still have this <u>same</u> HOLY SPIRIT who is wooing us to allow Him access into our own lives. Personally, I don't know why any of us would not want to grow in relationship with and be led by the HOLY SPIRIT!

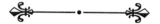

In April of this year, I was on Facebook with one of the women we met on the missions/ministry China trip with Marilyn Hickey in 2013 and messaging to her about an upcoming trip to Buenos Aires, Argentina. She had just been to a three-day Christian women's conference and hadn't planned to go on the Argentina trip. I wrote her that I didn't think we would be going either. Then in a flash-second—after we finished what we were writing to each other—a photograph of a flower <u>from Argentina</u> popped up on the screen! The name of the flower was "Victoriana!" **We both saw it at the same time.** That was when I decided to pray about going.

At the same time, I also wondered if that might have happened like it did because of the impartation of GOD's anointing that she had received at the women's conference. Still not positive that we were to go on this trip, I moved ahead with reservations anyway. Then I heard from the trip coordinator that a smaller group was going to be going on to Patagonia from Buenos Aires. More to pray about.

The night before the DEADLINE to get reservations in for my girls and I to go on to Patagonia; my daughter, Brenda, was texting her brother, Jason, about Patagonia. Jason was telling Brenda that Patagonia is considered the fly-fishing capital of the world! One of his strongest passions is fly-fishing. However, I had never heard of Patagonia.

The next morning, up popped a video on Facebook showing thousands of seabirds—Imperial Cormorants—that were nesting on a portion of coastline in Patagonia! As the images showed them from a distance above, I could see that they were all situated in the form of a DOVE! There were thousands of black and white birds sitting in their own little nesting places within a foot or so from one another, and <u>all of them together</u> filling in the shape of a dove—the sign of the Holy Spirit—stretching along the coastline. You could see the head, the beak and eyes; then down from the head, the wings stretched out. I couldn't help but think about what went into the process that the HOLY SPIRIT used bringing these seabirds in and sitting them all down **in the form of a dove** along <u>that</u> coastline of Patagonia, <u>then</u> having someone fly a video-drone over them, <u>then</u> getting that video on Facebook, and <u>then</u> putting me right in front of my computer to see it **<u>on the day</u> that I had to know whether or not the LORD wanted us to go!** Now I was <u>more than ready </u>to go <u>with high anticipation </u>for what He had waiting for us there!

JESUS died on the Cross to **provide <u>all</u>** of this—**the active daily involvement of the Holy Spirit**—for <u>us</u> which He demonstrated in His own life here on earth. In John 14:26, JESUS said, *"But the Helper, the Holy Spirit, whom the Father will send in My name, He will teach you all things, and bring to your remembrance all that I said to you."*

As for you, and as for me, does it not behoove each and every one of us to <u>bring</u> the HOLY SPIRIT into <u>everything</u> we endeavor to accomplish so that GOD can receive the GLORY for HIS manifested POWER being released into our lives, and JESUS can properly receive the REWARD for ALL HIS SUFFERING?

As our time to leave for Argentina got closer—with a long "Things to Do" list before us—I was being made aware in my spirit of the importance of engaging in spiritual warfare prayer <u>before</u> our departure. We were going into unfamiliar territory and no doubt would be encountering demonic forces that had not been confronted up to now, not by me at least.

Knowing there had been others who had gone before us and taken territories for the Kingdom of God, I thought perhaps I could find some clues as to how to pray concerning this trip to Argentina in one of Chuck Pierce's[36] books that was sitting on a table in my living room. The title of this book co-authored with Rebecca Wagner

---

[36] Chuck Pierce: President of **Global Spheres, Inc.**; known for his accurate prophetic gifting understanding the times and seasons in which we live.

Sytsema[37] is ***Prayers That Outwit the Enemy***. I opened to pages 70-71 with intentions to scan through the paragraphs for some helpful hints. It was to my <u>astonishment</u> that what I was reading was exactly what I was looking for! The type of praying that was being described on these pages came under the heading, *The Confrontation Prayer*. The main quote that touched my spirit is this: "God allows us to enter into this type of power encounter to show His power over territorial spirits to which a particular group of people has been in bondage. As God displays that His power is greater than that of a demonic structure, that structure begins to crumble and those who have been held captive by fear are then free to follow Christ."

Pierce and Sytsema go on to quote C. Peter Wagner's book, ***Confronting the Queen of Heaven***, where Wagner[38] gave a great exhortation on confrontation which he derived from the level of spiritual warfare that Paul must have had in mind when he wrote to the Ephesians (Ephesians 1:21). There are at least three very important things that the head (Jesus) is telling the body about spiritual warfare. Written from Wagner's personal experiences, I am quoting them below.

- **Stand against the wiles of the devil.** *Paul tells the Ephesians to put on the whole armor of God ("...that you may be able to stand against the wiles of the devil" Eph. 6:13). This is not a benign command. It is not something which is easy to do. The reason for this is that the devil is an awesome being. Paul, in the same epistle, calls him "the prince of the power of*

---

[37] Rebecca Sytsema: Director of **Children of** Destiny, freelance author and coauthor/editor of multiple Christen books.
[38] C. Peter Wagner: Christian theologian, missionary, writer, teacher, and church growth specialist.

the air" (Eph. 2:2.) It is hard for me to understand why some Christian leaders insist on trivializing Satan's power. Referring to him as a wimp or as a toothless lion only serves to embolden people to think they can get away with attacking the devil with a fly swatter. I suspect that by saying things like this, some well-intentioned believers are comparing the power of the devil to the power of God, and it is true that there is no contest between the two of them. But this is not the scenario at hand. We are not spectators watching a fight between God and demons. We are the ones whom God has designated to stand against the wiles of the devil. The head tells the body to do it, and clearly, the head is not going to do it for us.

- Engage in proactive spiritual warfare. In the letter to Ephesus Jesus says, "To him who overcomes, I will give to eat from the tree of life which is in the midst of the Paradise of God" (Rev. 2:7). The word "overcome," which Jesus repeats seven times, is nikao in the original Greek. It is a military word meaning "to conquer," in secular Greek, but, according to The New International Dictionary of New Testament Theology: "In the New Testament (nikao) almost always presupposes the conflict between God and opposing demonic powers" (Vol. 1, p.650). In other words, it means to do spiritual warfare.

- Declare God's wisdom to the principalities. Paul expresses to the Ephesians his burning desire that "the manifold wisdom of God might be made known by the church to the principalities and powers in the heavenly places" (Eph. 3:10). This is another one of the commands from the head of the body, and it explicitly says that the church should make this declaration to the powers in the invisible world. There are many interpretations as to what exactly this might mean, but one of them would be *that we declare the Gospel of the kingdom of God. The church, by deed and also by word, should remind the territorial spirits over places like Ephesus that the kingdom of God has invaded the kingdom of darkness beginning with the life, death, and resurrection of Jesus Christ. And that the god of this age will no longer blind the minds of unbelievers to the glorious Gospel of Christ in Ephesus, Turkey, Japan, Nepal, Calcutta, or in any other place. This kind of a declaration of war will predictably spark negative reactions and counterattacks from the forces of evil and the spiritual battle will be engaged. One of the major apostles of the extraordinary Argentine Revival, now in its seventeenth year, is evangelist Carlos Annacondia. In virtually every one of his meetings, he literally declares the wisdom of God to the devil and to any spiritual principalities that might be in the vicinity. Many times I have heard him do this in a very loud voice and with powerful anointing of the Holy Spirit. The title of his excellent book is:* Listen to Me, Satan! (*Creation House*). *When this war cry goes forth, night after night, things begin to happen. Demons manifest and are summarily dispatched, sick people are healed miraculously, and sinners literally run to the platform to get saved. More than two million have been born again in his campaigns so far.*

Pierce and Sytsema go on to write in their book that there are times when God will also call us into a confrontational type of warfare over demonic structures on a personal or family level, in which case the three points that were quoted above also apply.

I immediately ordered this book, *Listen to Me, Satan!* by Carlos Annacondia[39], which arrived within a few days. My full intention was to read the book at every opportunity afforded to me on the way to Argentina.

However, on the <u>third morning prior to departure</u>, I woke up with blurred vision! I couldn't even see to read my Bible. When I went onto my computer, I was seeing a shadow-line of print and another line of print below that one. It was extremely difficult to detect which line I was trying to focus on. With plans already in the making, itinerary in hand, I needed to rely on God's Grace and continue in Faith that He was going to take care of me! That condition never left but persisted throughout the entire trip to Buenos Aires, Argentina; Uruguay; and El Calafate in the Patagonia Region. However, my inability to see clearly didn't keep me from recognizing that there was still an **awesome move of the HOLY SPIRIT taking place in South America!**

The church we visited in Buenos Aires was an **on-fire** church—**Iglesia Rey del Reyes Church,** pastored by Claudio J. Freidzon[40] and his wife, Betty. As we sat through an evening service, Betty Freidzon was proclaiming the <u>truth of the Gospel non-stop</u>! Decrees and proclamations in the Spanish language were going out over the people as she barely paused long enough to take a breath in between! Beautiful people, brilliant colors, beautiful spirits, awesome **<u>praise and worship</u>**; and everything state-of-the-art! The people were showing **immense hunger and thirst for the things of GOD** and rushing to the front for prayer!

---

[39] Carlos Annacondia: Interdenominational crusade evangelist.
[40] Claudio J. Freidzon: Pastor and author of several books including *Holy Spirit, I Hunger for You.*

Even when we were far south of Buenos Aires in the small town of El Calafate, we walked into a little shop where the clerk had her Bible opened to Psalms on the counter. As I began to question her about JESUS, she apologetically gestured because she spoke only Portuguese. That didn't stop her! She ran out of the store across the cobblestone plaza to a different shop and came back with a young gentleman by the name of Roberto. Her name was Theresa. Roberto did speak English, and he shared with us that he is a pastor and he was there from a church in Buenos Aires on a 6-month mission trip with his wife and two children!

I ran over to Theresa's Bible and turned the pages to the Book of Acts, asking Roberto if he had received the Baptism of the HOLY SPIRIT with the evidence of speaking with other tongues? When he said yes, that he did speak with other tongues, we looked at each other and both said at the same time, "BROTHER and SISTER!" Then hugs and kisses! We shared things together for about the space of half an hour, and then I purchased a sweater coat from Theresa because I could tell how important it was for her to make this sale!

After returning home the HOLY SPIRIT showed me who He had me purchase the sweater coat for, a very kind woman who had volunteered to help my sister with some of her business obligations while I was away.

Within a few days of returning from the trip I noticed my left eye was drooping. Seeing with double-vision for the biggest share of the month of May was one thing, but having it put a dampener on daily activities required on a mission trip was another! We had traveled by ferry, buses, taxis, and domestic airlines, all the while I had to look straight down at my feet in order to see steps. **Praise the Lord**, I only crashed to the ground two times with little physical harm done, even though I did break a nail and a piece off my camera.

Now with my left eye obviously drooping, I decided to go to Prompt Care. From there, I was sent to the hospital. Each doctor I saw, sent me to another doctor; and each ran separate tests until I was being diagnosed with a condition I had never heard of called Myasthenia Gravis. It was a condition where the nerves stop signaling the muscles and, as this doctor was describing to me what it could progress into, I thought it sounded like the worst thing I had ever heard.

Even though I was hearing everything he was saying, it was as though what he was describing was <u>on a back burner</u> while at the same time, a Scripture was playing in my mind on *a front burner.*

> The Scripture was from Isaiah 41:10 (KJV): ***"Fear thou not for I am with thee; be not dismayed for I am thy God: I will strengthen thee; yea, I will help thee; yea, I will uphold thee with the right hand of my righteousness."***

<u>This is why</u> we need to study the Word and meditate on the Scriptures until they become an inner reservoir for the HOLY SPIRIT to draw from in times like this when we are going to need them the most.

<u>We also need to understand that any diagnosis is based upon current medical *fact*.</u>
<u>Healing is based upon TRUTH from the Word of God!</u>

When we continually confess that the Greater One is in us because the Word of GOD says, *"Greater is He that is in us than He that is in the world,"* we shouldn't be surprised when we experience things like this happening. The Greater One had risen up in my mind from a *heavenly standpoint* simultaneous to the report that was being spoken from the doctor's perspective.

From there, even further testing and more things being reported from MRI, ultra-sound, blood work-ups, and x-rays. I was being put on several different medications from all these test results, and then my cousin, Ron, called me from Colorado!

Remember cousin, Ron, from Chapter Seven? After relaying to Ron all the doctor reports, here's what Ronnie said: "**JUDY, IF I WERE YOU, I WOULD NEVER LET THOSE WORDS COME OUT OF MY MOUTH AGAIN AS LONG AS I LIVE—NOT EVEN A PORTION OF THEM!**" Then he added, "**DON'T LET THE DEVIL BACK YOU INTO A CORNER IN ORDER TO GET YOU TO SAY THEM EITHER!**"

Ron was right! I knew I had to **engage** in spiritual warfare because the battle was already raging, and all I had done was make a lot of noise. All the *talk* had done nothing to bring damage to the enemy. What it had done was ***divulge my position to the enemy***, and that position was lining up with the doctors' reports, findings, and recommendations. **Only GOD** has the true knowledge of our entire situation so we are <u>not</u> to *esteem* the doctors' reports over the Truth in God's Word!

Repeating reports, diagnoses, and opinions only serves to *keep us connected* to the illness because it is ONLY the BLOOD OF JESUS and the DNA in JESUS' BLOOD that separates the sickness <u>off</u> the people. The Word of God that says, ***"By His stripes we*** *were healed."* The Blood JESUS shed on the Cross has never lost its Power and serves as a sharp sword that *severs* all things pertaining to the curse off us!

Even the episodes that are described in the Bible can be powerful when we put ourselves in the same episodes. I had forgotten that just prior to our leaving on the trip to Argentina I had seen a vision of an empty row boat sitting at the edge of a body of water. I had no idea why I saw that, and I didn't say anything to anyone about it. However, upon hearing the news of this illness I had been diagnosed with, my ex-husband told me he was looking at it like JESUS' disciples when JESUS was in the boat with them. Gerald was seeing JESUS in the boat with me, and JESUS saying, "**We're going to the other side**," just like JESUS had said to those disciples.

After that **very strong advice from my cousin, Ron**, I determined to speak ONLY the Word of God throughout the rest of that day—Scripture after Scripture declaring that I had already been healed! By that night when I went to bed, I heard these words in my spirit, "**Finally, something solid to stand on.**" (I was getting there!)

I continued confessing the Word of God and praying in the spirit while being shown other things to decree out of my mouth such as: "I do not doubt today, neither do I doubt tomorrow." "Keep knocking the devil down with the Word until he can't get up anymore." When we commit to doing things GOD'S way, the HOLY SPIRIT comes alongside to help us!

When the devil tempted JESUS in the wilderness, JESUS responded with, *"It is written...."* With this as our example, we need also to say, "It is written" or "The Word says...*This light affliction is but for a moment."* In other words, call it a small thing and call it short-lived! Bringing our words into present tense we can say this:

"God's fury is going out like a whirlwind against my enemies, and I am being healed by the power of God!"

> Jeremiah 29:11 (KJV): *For I know the thoughts that I think toward you, saith the LORD, thoughts of peace, and not of evil, to give you an expected end.*

Correction came at times when I weakened in speaking the Word, and the HOLY SPIRIT conveyed to me that by talking the circumstances to my friends, I was keeping them on the ground with me. HE wants us to **soar and take others with us**, even taking doctors with us in healing teaching.

Just prior to one doctor appointment, I was hearing *similar* words to an old but popular song being sung in my spirit. "I love to tell the stories of JESUS and HIS GLORY, I love to tell the stories of JESUS and HIS LOVE!" It's time for all of us to play catch-up because too many in the body of Christ are lagging behind in TELLING the stories of Jesus. We are being moved into a new day of living in greater service, dedication, and hard work in the Kingdom of GOD; intense and extreme **ministering** because of the HOLY SPIRIT'S outpouring!

As we move further into the last of the last days, even as darkness is coming onto the earth to a degree of intensity beyond anything we have witnessed in our lifetime, the Church must become **one strong army**! It is time to "UP our game," listen to the Holy Spirit (and the prophets of old as well as those of today) as He leads us to His strategic instructions through their edification, warnings, and encouragements.

> Jeremiah 12:5 says, *"If you have run with the footmen and they have tired you out, then how can you compete with horses? If you fall down in a land of peace, how will you do in the thicket of the Jordan?"*
>
> In Proverbs 23:16, 18: *"And my inmost being will rejoice when your lips speak what is right. <u>Surely there is a future, and your hope will not be cut off</u>."*

As I read that Proverb, the symptoms were still with me. "When **is** this going to end?" was a question I muttered to myself when I didn't think anyone was listening. The HOLY SPIRIT heard me and said, "When you tell it to." That's right! I can give it a date! I had forgotten that!

I had received an invitation from a friend to come to an evening meeting on July 24th at The Hilton Inn. Rabbi Michael Zeitler[41] was to be ministering that evening with his wife, Lucy. Along with the invitation was a video of the Rabbi being interviewed by Sid Roth on the *"It's Supernatural"* television program! After viewing the video of Rabbi Zeitler's testimony of salvation and hearing that over 2,000 people had received healing when he was in Peru, I set the 24th as the date for my own healing to manifest! Then while in prayer that afternoon, I saw a vision of a man walking up to unlock my car door. But when he got to my car, he saw that it was already unlocked.

That evening, at the close of the meeting I went up for prayer. Giving a brief explanation of what the symptoms were, I told the

---

[41] Rabbi Michael Zeitler: Ministering through Spirit-filled, prophetic worship, revealing the supernatural and prophetic placement of Israel in these end times.

Rabbi, "It's serious!" He said, "I know it is!" He prayed for me and decreed that I was healed in the name of JESUS!

I had a dream that very same night that I was back in the meeting and walking up to the front of the room with both hands open. In the palm of each hand was a stack of pills. They were the main medications that had been prescribed to me, and I was **trading them in for my healing**! I was handing them over to a young man who was standing in the front of the room. I didn't know who he was or why he was in the dream, but he was standing off to the side of Rabbi Zeitler. I was saying, "If GOD doesn't heal me, I will die."

The next morning as I reflected on the dream, I thought because *faith is an action word*, if I continue to stay on the medicine, my *actions* would be saying I wasn't healed yet. So <u>when would I believe enough</u> to stop taking the pills? I will stop taking them NOW! If GOD gave me that dream—and I believed HE did—then I will go with the dream! That was the end of taking the medication, **and the end of every lying symptom of that disease**!

I had been on three different pills, three times a day, and the medicine had been keeping the symptoms at bay enough so that I was able to read Carlos Annacondia's book. However, one afternoon **prior to being prayed for**, I had skipped the pills because I was at a doctor's appointment from 3 p.m. to 9 p.m. By the end of the day, all the symptoms were back on me.

While in another doctor's office, I was told about a man who had been in the office just ahead of me who had the same thing they had diagnosed me with. He had stopped taking his medicine, and all the symptoms came right back on him!

When I stopped all the medication four weeks went by with no further symptoms! I had another appointment with the doctor who had initially diagnosed me. This time after running tests, I explained to him why I had stopped taking the medicine he had prescribed. I told him this wasn't my first rodeo because GOD had healed me of several things before as well as other members of my family. I shared with him about the Rabbi coming to Springfield and praying for me and about the dream I had that very night. Then further explanation about how the **Word of God** carries with it the very <u>power</u> of GOD to perform what is written in HIS WORD. I also shared a few quotes from the teachings of others who are being used in healing ministries.

In so many words, he concluded that either GOD had healed me or that it had gone into remission! He had no other explanation of the <u>normal</u> test results.

Three days later, I was back in our second meeting with Rabbi Michael Zeitler and Lucy testifying about my healing to this group that may have been three times larger in number than those who had attended the first meeting. This time Rabbi Zeitler prayed for me again and prophesied to me that from now on, anyone I pray for with this same condition will be healed by the power of GOD as well!

The next morning, I woke up hearing *loud and clear in my spirit*, **"YOUR FAITH HAS MADE YOU WHOLE!"** To me it sounded just like JESUS would have said it to the people HE healed when HE walked the earth Himself <u>over 2,000 years ago</u>!

He is still alive **IN US!**
HE is the same yesterday, today, and forever!
HALLELUJAH!! PRAISE HIS HOLY NAME!!!!

As we were going into the month of October I decided to revisit Carlos Annacondia's book, *Listen to Me, Satan!* It was then that I realized for the first time, the "Preface," **which also contained a most interesting testimony,** was written by <u>Claudio J. Freidzon</u>, pastor of the Buenos Aires church we had been in! As we become more aware of God's Grace in our lives—His desire to walk with us in all circumstances—it is such a joy to discover the threads He's used to demonstrate the extent of how much he Loves and Cares for us.

<u>Notes</u>:

1. Chuck D. Pierce and Rebecca Wagner Sytsema, *Prayers That Outwit the Enemy* **(Bloomington, Minnesota: Chosen Books, 2004) pp. 68-72. Used by permission.**
2. C. Peter Wagner, *Confronting the Queen of Heaven* (Colorado Springs, CO: Wagner Publications, 2001) pp. 31-35.
3. Carlos Annacondia, *Listen to Me, satan!* (Lake Mary, Florida: Charisma House, A Strang Company, 1998, 2008)

<u>Closing Personal Notes</u>:

Satan (the "great deceiver" and enemy who seeks to destroy every good thing and *kill* us) would have us believe that there are no consequences to our actions. Our own *basic human nature* carries his scar of *pride* and *independence*. Yet we are NOT helpless **spectators!**

Here are a few of my favorite "go to" Scriptures that remind me of WHO God has made me to BE.

- *"Before I formed you in the womb I knew you, and before you were born I consecrated you..."* Jeremiah 1:5
- *"For I know the plans I have for you,' declares the LORD, 'plans for welfare and not for calamity, to give you a future and a hope."* Jeremiah 29:11
- *"There is an appointed time for everything. And there is a time for every event under heaven—..."* Ecclesiastes 3:1-22
- *"And the LORD will continually guide you and satisfy your desire in scorched places and give strength to your bones; and you will be like a watered garden, like a spring of water, whose waters do not fail."* Isaiah 58:11
- *"Yet those who wait for the LORD will gain new strength; they will mount up with wings like eagles, they will run and not get tired, they will walk and not become weary."* Isaiah 40:31
- *"And we know that God causes all things to work together for good to those who Love God, to those who are called according to His purpose."* Romans 8:28
- *"And do not be conformed to this world, but be transformed by the renewing of your mind, so that you may prove what the will of God is, that which is good and acceptable and perfect."* Romans 12:2

As I complete the pages of this book, I am reminded of the Roman soldier, Cornelius. You may recall his story mentioned in Chapter One— <u>Know Your Divine Destiny</u>. EVEN THOUGH he was a *Roman/Gentile* he was **"a devout man and one who feared God...**

with all his household....and prayed to God always." God <u>knew</u> this man's heart and heard his <u>prayers!</u> Cornelius was an ordinary "working man" of his time. His soldier career must have offered him many physical, mental, emotional, <u>and spiritual</u> challenges. He may have been in battles, seen horrendous things, and suffered painful and life-threatening wounds. Yet this soldier ***believed*** and ***spoke*** to God in prayer, ***always.*** He and God were in constant communication! WHAT AN AMAZING EXAMPLE FOR US!

It is my greatest hope that, as you read this last page, you will be encouraged to *"...pray at all times in the Spirit...be on the alert with all perseverance and petition for all the saints...to make known with boldness the mystery of the Gospel..."* Ephesians 6:18-20.

My constant prayer for you—and me—is that together we will BE the AMBASSADORS of God we're meant to BE, proclaiming the **Gospel of Truth** and speaking in <u>boldness</u> with the Holy Spirit's inspiration. And, like the early Christians—Cornelius, the Apostles, and all the disciples of ***The Way of Jesus***—may the Hand of the Lord be with us with great numbers turning to the LORD as they come to BELIEVE. (Acts 11:21)

As we are, likewise, being **called to the greatest *battle in the history of the Church*** in **God's** <u>next season of **HARVEST**</u>, let us not be swayed to give any less than that which is required of us. We are called to be as steadfast and sure footed as was the early Church against the rulers of darkness and the powers and principalities of the air. May we be VICTORIOUS TOGETHER, A STRONG ARMY OF THE LORD, MIGHTY IN BATTLE!

Ministries and Reading Resources

Carlos Annacondia

Annacondia may well be the most effective citywide interdenominational crusade evangelist of all time. Making disciples is his focus. Like Billy Graham, Annacondia secures a broad base of interdenominational support from pastors and other Christian leaders…bringing men and women to faith in Jesus and into responsible membership in a local church. Like Dwight Moody and Billy Sunday he has had no formal academic theological training. Like Reinhard Bonnke and T. L. Osborne he features miracles, healings and deliverance from evil spirits in his meetings. It is Annacondia's intentional, premeditated, high-energy approach to spiritual warfare that is making a difference in Argentina and beyond. www.carlosannacondia.org

Rodney Howard-Browne

Drs. Rodney and Adonica Howard-Browne are the founders of *Revival Ministries International*, *The River at Tampa Bay Church*, *River Bible Institute*, *River School of Worship*, and *River School of Government* in Tampa, Florida. In December of 1987, Rodney, and his family moved from their native land, South Africa, to the United States—**called by God as missionaries from Africa to America**. The Lord had spoken through Rodney in a word of prophecy and declared: "As America has sown missionaries over the last 200 years, I am going to raise up people from other nations to come to the United States of America. I am sending a mighty revival to America." Every soul matters and every salvation is a victory for the kingdom of God! With a passion for souls and a passion to revive and mobilize the body of Christ, Drs. Rodney and Adonica continue to preach the Gospel of Jesus Christ in the U.S. and around the world. www.revival.com

Juanita Bynum

Dr. Juanita Bynum has had an interesting faith journey. She has been a mainstay staple on the *Trinity Broadcasting Network* for the last few years. In addition to her television ministry she has traveled the world being an inspiring preacher and teacher at many revivals and conferences throughout the United States and abroad. She has been elevated to the position of Bishop, by Bishop Neil C. Ellis, presiding bishop of Global United Fellowship which embraces Churches, Ministries, Fellowships, and Pastors who acknowledge, accept and submit to Jesus Christ as Savior and Lord. Bynum is also a Platinum Gospel recording artist, *New York Times* Best Selling author, actress, and empowerment coach. www.juanitabynum.com

Merlin Carothers...

Methodist Pastor and author of books such as *Prison to Praise, Power in Praise, Praise Works, From Fear to Faith* and *Bringing Heaven into Hell*. Carothers' life was devoted to public service from Lieutenant Colonel, U.S. Army, to founder of the **Foundation of Praise**—an outreach ministry called to get free books into every state and federal prison in America, and into as many city and county jails as possible. This ministry continues after Merlin's passing in November, 2013, also sowing books into military, hospitals, crisis pregnancy centers, and missionary projects around the world.

Mark Chironna

Bishop Chironna is a passionate preacher of the Gospel of Christ whose message is that the wholeness of the Gospel leads to the experience of wholeness in our life...as we continually seek Christ. He has a father's heart for emerging generations and serves as the Presiding Bishop of **Legacy Edge Alliance**, a worldwide fellowship of senior apostolic leaders and churches. Bishop Chironna is regarded as an influential leader whose global reach, clarion voice, and prophetic insight are respected by leaders and followers alike. He holds multiple advanced degrees in theology and psychology, and is the founder and senior pastor of **Church on the Living Edge** in Orlando, Florida...encouraging every Believer to BECOME the most effective "you" that God has intended. www.markchironna.com

Kim Clement

Born in South Africa, Clement traveled many physical and spiritual miles to finally accept the position/destiny God gave him. In 1981, Kim came to the United States to attend Christ for the Nations. Between 1981-1991, Kim traveled throughout the United States, returning 5 times a year to assist at *Durban Christian Center* in Durban, South Africa. In 1991, Kim moved with his family to the USA. After years of travel and ministering, Kim started *The Warriors of the New Millennium,* an outreach based in Detroit, Michigan that focused on uplifting the wounded people within the City; this eventually spread throughout the United States. Kim now resides in Southern California with his family and is pioneering a new online prophetic outreach. www.kim-clement.com

Kenneth and Gloria Copeland

The Copelands are leaders of the Charismatic Movement, public speakers and televangelists. They are founders of *Kenneth Copeland Ministries* (KCM) advocating daily application of the "Word of God", meaning the BIBLE. This teaching ministry focuses on faith, love, healing, prosperity and restoration through diverse media, such as television, books, CD and DVD. KCM's motto is JESUS IS LORD— based upon Romans 10:9. www.kcm.org

Andre Crouch

An American Gospel singer, songwriter, arranger, record producer and pastor passed from this earthly life on January 8,

2015. He continues to hold the title of "the father of modern gospel music" by many who honor and respect his music ministry to the world. He may be best known for his song: "The Blood Will Never Lose Its Power," "My Tribute (To God Be the Glory)" and "Soon and Very Soon."

David Du Plessis

South African-born Pentecostal minister, Du Plessis is considered one of the main founders of the charismatic movement, in which the Pentecostal experience of Baptism with the Holy Spirit spread to non-Pentecostal churches worldwide. Born to missionary parents he accepted Christ at the age of 11 and received the baptism of the Holy Spirit accompanied by speaking in tongues at the age of 18. Ordained in 1928 God led him to the United States and a focus on ecumenical efforts. His autobiography—*The Spirit Bade Me Go*—continues to inspire peoples of all Christian denominations. Often recognized as "Mr. Pentecost" DuPlessis transitioned from this earth February 2, 1987.

The Elijah List

http://www.elijahlist.com...called to transmit around the world, in agreement with Holy Scripture, fresh daily prophetic "manna" from the Lord, regarding the days in which we live.

Claudio J. Freidzon

Dr. Claudio Freidzon, together with his wife Betty, is the senior pastor and founder of *King of Kings Church* in Buenos Aires, Argentina, which today has over 30,000 active members. He has preached the Word of God in gigantic meetings held on the five continents reaching over 10 million people with the message of the gospel. Freidzon has written several internationally best-selling books including *Holy Spirit, I Hunger for You*, translated into nine languages, and the devotional *From Glory to Glory*. His charity organization—*Operation Life*—is an outreach whose vision is to reach the lost through charity work and the gospel. Through his Foundation, he has also established a radio station, FM Gospel...and the *Buenos Aires Christian School*, a bilingual school promotes Christian values and enrichment of spiritual life as it trains the next generations of leaders that will make a difference in society. Many testimonies of supernatural miracles, ministries restored and lives renewed by the glorious presence of the Holy Spirit are the evidence of God's grace upon his life and ministry. www.claudiofreidzon.com

Grace World Outreach Church/Grace Church...Granite City, IL & Maryland Heights, MO

Founder, Pastor Ron Tucker sought God's plan for his future and became a youth pastor which quickly grew to over 1500 people of every age. In 1980, the church moved into a modest building and prepared for what God would do next. Since then the church has grown in size, facilities and spirit. Thousands of lives and eternities have been changed as the focus remains on loving God and serving people—One Church and now two campuses. At Grace Church, we believe in the same Biblical truths that have been held sacred since the time of Christ. We affirm God's Truths that are unchangeable and encourage everyone to grow in their personal relationship with Christ. www.gracestl.org

Billy Graham

Evangelist Billy Graham took Christ literally when He said in Mark 16:15, *"Go ye into all the world and preach the Gospel to every creature."* He has preached the Gospel to more people in live audiences than anyone else in history. As he approached 95 years of age, Mr. Graham recorded a new video message, called "The Cross," which has been made available for use in homes and churches as a tool for sharing the Gospel. He has written 33 books, including his autobiography "Just As I Am," (1997) and the most recent "Where I Am: Heaven, Eternity, and Our Life Beyond" (2015). www.billygraham.org.

Pastor Paul Griffis

Biblical Advisor and Teacher, *Sounds of Life Foursquare*, Springfield, Illinois…Pastoring sheep, giving biblical counsel, missionary work, evangelist, and Bible teacher, husband and father, and grandfather.

Ron Hamilton

…….called by **vision** to minister God's Word—*life*—victory—and freedom to those incarcerated in prisons and jails.

Marilyn Hickey

Over 35 years ago, Marilyn Hickey accepted God's Call on her life to *'cover the earth with His Word'* (Isaiah 11:9). In the early years she couldn't imagine what that would mean. Today, she is a highly sought after international speaker and her teachings on healing and the Bible have broken records in several countries for the largest public meetings ever held in that nation's history. She is one of God's *bridge builders* reaching out to people of all cultures and religious backgrounds, especially Muslims and continues to lead ministry missions trips around the world. Co-founder of *Orchard Road Christian Center*. www.marilynandsarah.org

Joan Hunter

Since the age of 12, when Joan dedicated her heart to the Lord, she has faithfully served Him. As a compassionate minister, dynamic teacher, accomplished author, and anointed healing evangelist it is her desire to see the body of Christ set free in their body, mind, soul, spirit and finances. Her focus is to train and equip believers to take the healing power of God beyond the 4 walls of the church and into the 4 corners of the earth! Being sensitive to the Holy Spirit, Joan speaks prophetically in the services, releasing personal and corporate prophetic ministry to those in attendance. She lovingly credits her parents, *The Happy Hunters*, Charles and Frances, with being two of God's inspiring influences in her life. www.joanhunter.org

Prophetess Mary Johnson-Gordon

Mary L. Johnson-Gordon is an ordained Elder in the Office of Prophet, and Carrier of God's word to His people, equipped with a special anointing to execute God's will through Healings, Miracles, Signs and Wonders. After many encounters with God and the God-Kind—including Supernatural transport into other dimensions and seeing Paradise—she is an End Time Prophet, and an Apostolic Preacher/Teacher prepared for teaching God's Way, developing and instructing God's People for another *dimension of service*. Blessed by her heritage as a Native American of the Haliwa Saponi Tribe of North Carolina, her *call* is to the Nations. To hear her speak or read her books—*Tell My People the Unalterable, Inconvenient Truths*, *Insights: God's Use of Earthly Inhabitants for His Kingdom Purposes* and *Revealing Divine Mysteries of the Lord of Mercy*—is to better know God, His Ways, and His Covenant with His People. Prophetess Mary continues to announce the Lord's messages on her website: www.maryjohnsongordon.com.

Sandra Kennedy

Dr. Sandra Kennedy is the founder and president of *Sandra Kennedy Ministries®*, as well as the founder and Senior Pastor of *Whole Life Ministries®*. http://www.sandrakennedy.org Under the inspiration of God, Pastor Sandra established *The Healing Center*, a wonderful place where the Word of God is exalted, the healing power of God is manifested and the love and compassion of Christ is demonstrated. She was given a mandate by God to "grow up the Body of Christ and teach them victory", addressing the whole man: spirit, soul, and body, authoring numerous books, including, *Preparations for a Move of God*, and *Hope for the Heart*.

Thomas Kinkade

Kinkade is known as "The Painter of Light" and is possibly one of the most admired and critiqued artists of our time. He explained that the focus of his *art* placed emphasis on the value of simple pleasures and that his intent was to communicate inspirational, life-affirming messages through his paintings. He was a self-described "devout Christian" and believed he gained his inspiration from his religious beliefs and that his work was intended to contain a larger moral dimension. He also said that his goal as an artist was to touch people of all faiths and to bring a sense of peace into their lives through the images he created. Many pictures contain specific chapter-and-verse allusions to Bible passages. Kinkade passed into new life April 6, 2012.

Kathryn Kuhlman

Author of *I Believe In Miracles*, Kuhlman was one of the most well-known healing ministers and leader in Pentecostalism in the world between 1940 and 1970s. Kuhlman was often heard disclaiming any personal responsibility for healing, saying it originated with the power of God. She spoke of an anointing that came over her as difficult to explain. "These things are supernatural," she said. "That's the reason it's so hard for the natural mind to comprehend... I am completely taken over by the Holy Spirit—just completely." Since healing came second to salvation in her ministry, the *Kathryn Kuhlman Foundation* still exists today—after her death in 1976—with inspiration and helps to reach as many people with the gospel as possible. www.kathrynkuhlman.com

Don Moen

Don Moen is an American singer-songwriter, pastor and producer of Christian worship music. He attended *Oral Roberts University* and became a *Living Sound* musician for *Terry Law Ministries* traveling with Law for 10 years. Moen produced 11 volumes for the *Hosanna!Music* series of worship albums. His first album under his own name, *Worship with Don Moen* was released in 1992. In December 2007 he started *The Don Moen Company* and acquired *MediaComplete*, the church software company that created *MediaShout*. Moen became a radio host for *Don Moen & Friends* in 2009. He received a <u>Dove Award</u> for his work on the musical **<u>God with Us</u>** in addition to amassing nine nominations for his songs and continues to be a prolific songwriter and encourager to many talented musicians.

Watchman Nee

At the moment of his salvation—at age seventeen—his plans for his future were entirely abandoned. He testified, "From the evening I was saved, I began to live a new life, for the life of the eternal God had entered into me." Later, when he was called by the Lord to carry out His commission, he adopted the English name *Watchman* and the Chinese name *To-sheng*, which means "the sound of a watchman's rattle," because he considered himself to be a watchman raised up to sound out a warning call in the dark night. www.watchmannee.org

In his teaching series titled: <u>The Spiritual Man</u>, Nee presents the workings of the human spirit and soul and body. The book aims at delivering people from the tyranny of self-life with its carnality and from the domination of the passions and lusts of the flesh—with the full salvation of Christ. It is not to be taken as a manual but as a guide to true spirituality. *Thus, it will be realized that in Thy light, shall we see light* (Psalm 36.9).

T. L. Osborn

A world missionary evangelist, statesman, teacher, author, publisher, linguist, designer, pianist and administrator, Osborn was best known for his mass-miracle ministry to millions of unreached people in over 90 nations. His focus was to Proclaim Christ and then Pray for miracles as proof Jesus is alive. His ministry continues—after his death in February, 2013—as the Lord remains present, alive and available to us all. Osborn's books, *God's Love Plan*, *The Good Life* and *The Message That Works* continue to lift people to positive Faith and super-living. His daughter, Dr. LaDonna C. Osborn, leads this ministry forward today. www.osborn.org.

Chuck Pierce

Charles D. "Chuck" Pierce serves as President of *Global Spheres, Inc.* (GSI) in Corinth, Texas. This is an apostolic, prophetic ministry that is being used to gather and mobilize the worshipping Triumphant Reserve throughout the world.

Chuck also serves as President of *Glory of Zion International Ministries*, a ministry that aligns Jew and Gentile. He is known for his accurate prophetic gifting which helps direct nations, cities, churches and individuals in understanding the times and seasons in which we live. Chuck has a degree in Business from Texas A&M, Master's work in Cognitive Systems from the University of North Texas, and a D. Min. from the Wagner Leadership Institute. Pierce has authored and co-authored over seventeen ministry books. www.gloryofzion.org

Janice Roth

Janice had a dramatic encounter with the Lord in December 1975. Her pastor asked her to start teaching a Sunday school class in March 1976 and the class grew. From there, teaching put her before many groups; *Aglow*, speaking at Women's Ministry Groups, and starting Bible study groups. One of those groups became a church in 1978. In January 1987 the Lord impressed upon her, as she was reading about Marilyn Hickey's upcoming trip, that she was to go. Being a school teacher, she didn't know how she'd get off work, she didn't have the finances, and she didn't have a passport. She had missed the cut off date, but it all came together in 3 weeks and she traveled with *Marilyn Hickey Ministries* to the Philippines and China. This was a large group of 150 doing ministry in Hong Kong, including smuggling Bibles into Communist China and doing door-to-door evangelism in the Philippines. Janice went on to receive her diploma from Rhema Bible Training College and is still teaching, mentoring others, and involved in an intercessory prayer group.

Thurman Scrivner

Thurman Scrivner was born in Texas and raised in a great Christian family. In church since birth, he was raised a Southern Baptist and became a Christian at the age of 11. Today, Thurman teaches God's Word and the promises given to us *"... that with all boldness they may speak Thy Word, by stretching forth thine hand to heal; and that signs and wonders may be done by the name of thy holy child Jesus"* (Acts 4:29-30)

He was just an average Christian growing up, attending church services, and Bible studies. When he returned from a tour of duty in Vietnam, from 1964-1965, he went to college to study engineering. Upon graduation, he secured a position as an engineering instructor for Braniff Airlines, teaching the systems on four-engine jets to pilots and engineers. Following this teaching career, Thurman became a commercial pilot and flew for Seaboard World Airlines, out of New York City, and for a German airline while living in Germany. After the German carrier filed bankruptcy, he came back to the U.S. and became a simulator instructor for American Airlines. One year later, he went to work for a large corporation as a regional engineer, designing equipment and managing building projects all over the country and abroad. During his 29 year tenure with them, Thurman also served as a Bible teacher and deacon and held many other offices in his church. Then the Lord "promoted" him out of the work force and catapulted him into the ministry full time at *The Living Savior Ministries* in Texas. www.tlsm.org

Nasir Sidikki

...at the age of thirty-four (1987) Siddiki experienced a life-threatening bout with shingles which he testifies led to his conversion from Islam to Christianity. In May 1997, Siddiki graduated from Rhema Bible Training College, founded by Kenneth E. Hagin, and received an honorary doctorate from the American Bible College and Seminary in Oklahoma City, Oklahoma where he taught a course in Biblical Economics. In 1998 Dr. Siddiki went into full-time ministry and started a ministry called *Wisdom Ministries*. His desire is to "teach God's Word all over the world and equip God's leaders with wisdom". www.wisdomministries.org

John Sherrell

John and his wife Elizabeth are Christian writers. They have co-authored a number of best-selling books, including: *God's Smuggler* with Brother Andrew, *The Hiding Place* with Corrie ten Bloom, and *The Cross and the Switchblade* with David Wilkerson. In their early writing years they were freelance writers. Then in 1970 they founded a publishing company, **Chosen Books**, dedicated to developing new Christian writers. Their first title was *Born Again* by Charles Colson. When John was a young reporter for *Guideposts* magazine, he was a skeptic when it came to *speaking in tongues* and the Baptism with the Holy Spirit. He set out to gather information about this strange occurrence that was happening all over the country, determined to retain his objectivity while digging out the facts. What he found changed his life and the lives of many others who read his inspired book, *They Speak With Other Tongues*. www.elizabethsherrel.com

Steve Shultz

Steve Shultz is the founder and publisher of ***The Elijah List*** the non-denominational Christian prophetic website www.elijahlist.com named from the Old Testament prophet, Elijah—"called to transmit around the world, in agreement with Holy Scripture, a fresh daily prophetic *manna* from the Lord regarding the days in which we live." Shultz had his first prophetic dream in 1984 and spent much of the 1980's and 1990's learning to hear God's voice. His first book, ***Can't You Talk Louder, God*** details a lot of his prophetic journey. In 1994, God released him to prophesy to others and he's been doing it ever since. When Steve ministers on the prophetic, his purpose is not only to encourage others with this prophetic gift, but to train them on the lavish grace and mercy given to us by Jesus Christ.

Lester Sumrall

Sumrall states that his ministry began when, at the age of seventeen, his doctor wrote out his death certificate. That night God gave him a vision of a coffin on one side of his bed and a Bible on the other. He had a choice—either preach the gospel or die of tuberculosis that night. Sumrall decided to preach the Gospel. He was healed and within three weeks packed his bag, left home and hit the evangelistic trail. For the next 65 years, his ministry grew rapidly moving from the back woods of the Deep South to traveling the world with the internationally known Bible teacher, Howard Carter. By 1957 he founded LeSEA, a ministry that continues to produce a quarterly magazine, books, study guides, television and radio stations that reach over ninety percent of the world's population. In 1987 Sumrall and his ministry family established *LeSEA Global Feed the Hungry* providing funds that feed millions of believers around the globe. www.lesea.com

Rebecca Wagner Sytsema

REBECCA currently serves as Director of **Children of Destiny**, and works as a freelance author and editor. She has coauthored eight Christian books to date. She works from home where she is first and foremost mom to three great boys: Nicholas (16, full-syndrome non-verbal ASD), Samuel (14, moderate ASD), and Trey (typically developing 10-year-old). Rebecca and husband Jack firmly hold to the belief that the most powerful intervention we have brought into our sons' lives has been to give them over to God and allow Him to order our steps. Although the path has been a difficult one, we have seen steady progress as God works new miracles day by day. God has yet to disappoint us in any area with which we have fully trusted Him! www.childrenofdestiny.org

Trinity Broadcasting Network

TBN is the world's largest religious television network and America's most watched faith channel...offering 24 hours of commercial-free inspirational programming that appeals to people in a wide variety of Protestant, Catholic and Messianic Jewish denominations...with Praise and

Worship... faith-based interviews and testimonials...and News and World events. www.tbn.org

C. Peter Wagner

Wagner is a Christian theologian, missionary, writer, teacher, and church growth specialist best known for his controversial writings on spiritual warfare. He has served as Professor of Church Growth at the *Fuller Theological Seminary's* School of World Missions until his retirement in 2001. Wagner was the president of *Global Harvest Ministries* from 1993 to 2011 and is currently the chancellor emeritus of *Wagner Leadership Institute*, which serves to train leaders to join in a movement known as the *New Apostolic Reformation*, an organization Wagner also helped to found. He is currently the vice-president of Global Spheres, Inc. He is the author of more than 70 books including *Confronting the Powers: How the New Testament Church Experienced the Power of Strategic-Level Spiritual Warfare* and *Engaging the Enemy*. www.globalharvest.org

Smith Wigglesworth

Wigglesworth was a British Evangelist and Faith Healer often referred to as "the Apostle of Faith." He was one of the pioneers of the Pentecostal revival that occurred in the 20th Century. Without human refinement and education he was able to tap into the infinite resources of God to bring Divine Grace to multitudes—thousands came to Christian Faith in his meetings, hundreds were healed of serious illnesses and diseases as supernatural signs followed his ministry. His deep

Faith in God's Word continues to be an example for believers of the Gospel today. www.smithwigglesworth.com

David Wilkerson

Called to New York in 1958 to minister to gang members and drug addicts—as told in the best-selling book, *The Cross and the Switchblade*—he returned there in 1987 and founded the *Times Square Church*, the place he calls "the crossroads of the world." As pastor, he faithfully led this congregation, delivering powerful biblical messages that encourage righteous living and complete reliance on God. His burden for the *lost* of the city increased and gave birth to *Teen Challenge*—a nationwide ministry to reach out to people with life controlling habits. This ministry's Bible-based recovery program reaches out to addicts, gang members and abandoned children on ghetto streets; traveling the globe to raise up *Teen Challenge centers* and preach the gospel to the poorest people in impoverished nations throughout the world. This ever-expanding ministry—birthed, operated and sustained by the Holy Spirit—grew into *World Challenge, Inc.* which now supports the crusades, ministers' conferences, church planting efforts, etc. everywhere. A car accident took the physical life of David Wilkerson on April 27, 2011. However, the ministry God began in him continues to proclaim the love of God around the world and to provide for the poor, as instructed in the Scriptures in Matthew 25:34-46 and James 1:27. www.worldchallenge.org

Women's Aglow

Aglow International is a Kingdom Movement committed to seeing God's will done on earth as it is in Heaven. Millions of women have been mobilized into a company of warriors, champions, and global leaders of significance...establishing powerful Kingdom Communities founded on the fullness of Christ in every nation of the world...empowering people to develop resources that enable them to take advantage of all that God is releasing from Heaven...forming apostolic teams that demonstrate the power of Heaven in the darkest places of earth...and cultivating a worldwide presence that creates an atmosphere of celebration, impartation, and restoration. www.aglow.org

Rabbi Michael Zeitler

Rabbi Zeitler, and his wife Lucy, minister through Spirit-filled and prophetic worship. Michael has been on Sid Roth's program *It's Supernatural*, sharing how he's seen thousands healed through the anointed "Shofar" blast. He also has an amazing ministry that reveals the supernatural and prophetic placement of Israel and its impact upon the end times.

CPSIA information can be obtained
at www.ICGtesting.com
Printed in the USA
FFOW01n2307080916
27503FF